FROM DRIFT TO *SHIFT*

Praise for
FROM DRIFT TO *SHIFT*

"Miller nails it with how to change your work and personal life so that you find meaning, balance, and happiness."

—**Peter O'Donnell**, Investor, Private Equity

"Jody is the Studs Terkel of our time."

—**Kristen Johnson**, NBC Television

"The stories in *From Drift to Shift* are like Ted Talks. You will be inspired to follow your own dreams and desires. There are no roadblocks."

—**Ray Bourhis**, Partner, Attorney

"You can easily follow the roadmap in *From Drift to Shift* to find your true place in the world. Miller lays it out, with amazing stories to support her years of professional experience."

—**Christie Balcolm Oppliger**, Transamerica Financial

"No one knows how to get to the heart of someone's story and help them see what matters better than Miller."

—**Johnny "Love" Metheny**, Entrepreneur

"The stories in *From Drift to Shift* probe the meanings and motivations that guide us and keep us going."

—**Dalton Delan**, PBS Television

"If you want to find real happiness in your work, Jody is the best at showing you how."

—**Allison Miller**, Head of Human Resources, JMPG

"Everyone should own a copy of this book. Whether you are a CEO or stay-at-home parent, this book will help you find your way in the world."

—**Greg Curhan**, Co-Founder & President, Merriman, Curhan Ford

"The stories in this book get to the heart of work and life. You will be motivated to pursue what matters."

—**Rick Berry**, CEO

"Inspiring examples of Jody connecting people and encouraging them to strive for more, leading to a life of peace and happiness."

—Larry Carpenter, M.D.

"If you haven't shifted already, *From Drift to Shift* will help you move into the authentic life and right livelihood we all deserve. Get inspired by Jody and the stories she weaves together."

—Jennifer Chapin, Co-Founder, Stinson Brands

"Jody Miller's gracefully narrated compilation of true life stories reminds us all that our personal and joyful destiny is within our reach. We need only to shake off the ennui, if not outright fear, we've slowly embraced in our adult lives, and embrace the fact that happiness has been patiently waiting for us all along."

—Ann Hough, Audit Manager, California State University Chancellor's Office

"Jody is an ace both on and off the court. The pieces in *From Drift to Shift* are nothing short of dynamic, inspiring storytelling that make you pause and seek out what is truly important in your own life. It's not whether you win or lose but how you play the game...the game of life.

—Mandy Aguero, Recruiter

"Jody's stories give us the opportunity to take a step back and reflect on our own lives. There is always something to be grateful for; we can all be inspired to build a better life."

—Nathalie Tancrede, Executive Director of Artisan Business Network

"Miller helps the reader discover America's Cup tactician-like skills in sensing SHIFTS and exploiting them in everyday life."

—Jeff Heely, Agro Vision

"When life gives you lemons, sometimes you need help to make the lemonade. *From Drift to Shift* can provide the ingredients you need."

—Lee Bailey, Owner, LeeB Productions

ALSO BY JODY B. MILLER

HIRED! In 2017
Hired! Expert Advice from a Leading Wall Street Recruiter
No Time for Love – a Novel
The Perfect Gift

To receive updates about Jody's schedule, blog, and new book releases,
please connect at http://www.jodybmiller.com
http://www.fromdrifttoshift.com

FROM DRIFT TO
SHIFT

*How Change Can Bring True
Meaning and Happiness
to Your Work and Life*

JODY B. MILLER

NEW YORK

NASHVILLE • MELBOURNE • VANCOUVER

FROM DRIFT TO *SHIFT*
How Change Can Bring True Meaning and Happiness to Your Work and Life

Published in New York, New York, by Morgan James Publishing. Morgan James is a trademark of Morgan James, LLC. www.MorganJamesPublishing.com

The Morgan James Speakers Group can bring authors to your live event. For more information or to book an event visit The Morgan James Speakers Group at www.TheMorganJamesSpeakersGroup.com.

ISBN 978-1-68350-292-0 paperback
ISBN 978-1-68350-293-7 eBook
ISBN 978-1-68350-294-4 hardcover
Library of Congress Control Number: 2016917089

Cover Design by:
Megan Whitney
megan@creativeninjadesigns.com

Interior Design by:
Bonnie Bushman
The Whole Caboodle Graphic Design

In an effort to support local communities, raise awareness and funds, Morgan James Publishing donates a percentage of all book sales for the life of each book to Habitat for Humanity Peninsula and Greater Williamsburg.

Get involved today! Visit
www.MorganJamesBuilds.com

DEDICATION

To my Dad.
You have always been my biggest fan.

TABLE OF CONTENTS

FOREWORD

by Author and CEO, Brad Feld

CEO, Venture Capitalist, Entrepreneur,
Bestselling Author, Marathoner

We all strive for success, but life often gets in the way and interferes with our grand plan. We go into turbo work mode to keep ourselves extra busy thinking we will find success. We follow the perfect plan someone else has laid out for us. But then it doesn't work out. When that happens, we have to make a shift in order to move forward.

While we occasionally know what shift to make, more often it confronts us and smacks us in the forehead. Regardless of circumstance or timing, we have to embrace change in order to find true meaning and happiness in our lives.

I've had my share of successes and failures throughout my professional career and personal life. While success can feel great, the failures can feel emotionally crippling. Periods of success can also be unfulfilling, resulting in confusion, anxiety, or even depression.

Regardless of our profession or relentless pursuit of our dreams, we often face internal struggles. These struggles can be forced upon us by accidents, emotional setbacks, physical health, or circumstances outside our control. Yet, we suffer.

Could it be that in making our way through suffering, we find a way out the other side? A way that is new, fresh, and better than before? I've suffered many times as an adult and through each phase of suffering, have learned about myself and come out of my struggle with more optimism.

There come multiple points in life when we have to make a shift in order to find true happiness and purpose, regardless of what others think. Whether you are a CEO or a stay-at-home parent, the stories in *FROM DRIFT to SHIFT* will inspire you toward an optimism that comes from facing your demons, your challenges, and the roadblocks along your path. In *FROM DRIFT to SHIFT*, you will learn about inspirational people who have found their way through hard times and struggles, emphasizing a belief in other outcomes.

Jody and I met many years ago when she was an Investment Banker and I was a Managing Director at SOFTBANK Technology Ventures. We had media and technology backgrounds which gave us instant common ground. While we each became authors later in life, Jody went on to Executive Recruiting and Strategic Consulting and I continued on the investment path with my role at Foundry Group and Techstars.

I deeply enjoyed the stories in this book. I was amazed at how each person worked through their shift on a path to finding their own bliss. The people in *FROM DRIFT to SHIFT* have found passion, laid it all on the line, and came out on top in their lives. They have gained empathy and a sense of self that cannot be destroyed.

My wish for you is for happiness to be your path and for love be your guide. You will find both in *FROM DRIFT to SHIFT*.

—**Brad Feld**, Boulder, Colorado

About Brad

Brad has been an early stage investor and entrepreneur since 1987. Prior to co-founding Foundry Group, he co-founded Mobius Venture Capital and, prior to that, founded Intensity Ventures. Brad is also a co-founder of Techstars.

In addition to his investing efforts, Brad has been active with several non-profit organizations and currently is chair of the National Center for Women & Information Technology, co-chair of Startup Colorado, and on the board of Path Forward. Brad is a nationally-recognized speaker on the topics of venture capital investing and entrepreneurship and writes the widely read blogs Feld Thoughts, Startup Revolution, and Ask the VC.

Brad holds Bachelor of Science and Master of Science degrees in Management Science from the Massachusetts Institute of Technology. Brad is also an avid art collector and long-distance runner. He has completed 23 marathons as part of his mission to finish a marathon in each of the 50 states.

ACKNOWLEDGMENTS

The perspective offered in this book is for you, the reader, to experience your work and life in a way that gives you balance, meaning, and happiness on a daily basis. This counsel is supported by 30+ years of professional experience, combined with poignant examples of amazing people's transformative stories.

The accurate and meaningful telling of these stories involves each person's willingness to be thoughtful, reflective, honest, and open.

Putting these experiences together so that you, the reader, can follow a fluid path to self-discovery, takes more than a writer; it takes a varied and cohesive team.

I would like to give you a short description of the incredible people whose journeys are woven throughout this book. Some have drifted initially, yet all have experienced significant *shifts* in their lives and, through these shifts, have become who they are meant to be.

- Andy Wirth: President and CEO of Squaw Valley and Alpine Meadows Ski Resorts, philanthropist, and extreme athlete.
- Jerry Colonna: CEO of Reboot, executive coach, venture capitalist, and enlightenment seeker.

- Sloan Walsh: Woman of endless faith, parent education teacher, and amazing mother of three.
- Manoj Chalam: Ph.D., Chemical Engineer, CEO, Hindu deity art collector, co-founder of Vivekodayam.org (a nonprofit organization focused on raising knowledge and wisdom), teacher of Hindu and Buddhist archetypes, and avid table tennis player.
- Serita and Reid Cox: Co-Founders and leaders of iFoster.org, collectors of unique cultural keepsakes, mountain adventurers, and the first to help kids who have been left behind.
- Darren Quinn: Talented, in-demand artist with paintings displayed on Television program sets and famous restaurants; water adventurer, sudden paraplegic, and friend to all.
- The Achuar People: Friendly, indigenous tribe living deep in the heart of the Amazon Rain Forest, believers in dreams, and lovers of Mother Earth.
- Emilee Garfield: Two-time cancer survivor, movement educator, and certified wellness coach.

Each of these individuals has overcome major struggles, doubts, and obstacles; and yet, through it all, has discovered why, when, and how to shift their lives to live each day with passion, meaning, and fullness. I am so grateful they were willing to share their inspirational stories, regardless of how humble they believe them to be. I thank them for being sources of incentive and inspiration to the many readers who will learn from them.

Brad Feld: Entrepreneur, investor, venture capitalist, bestselling author and marathon runner extraordinaire, who wrote the foreword to *FROM DRIFT to SHIFT,* has helped many entrepreneurs realize their place in the world through numerous start-ups and ventures. Now, he will help even more through his eloquent perspective and kind words in *FROM DRIFT to SHIFT.*

I am thankful to Terry Whalin, Acquisitions Editor at Morgan James Publishing, whom I first met at the San Francisco Writer's Conference. He saw my vision and valued this book from the beginning, helping to shepherd it through the publishing house.

The whole team at Morgan James played an integral role in producing and distributing the important messages in this book, and I am grateful for their belief, commitment, and dedication to the entire process.

I give special thanks to Megan Malone, Managing Editor at Morgan James, who had just the right touch and timing.

Thank you to my conceptual and copy editors, who were tried and true with every technical and thematic element of this book.

Heartfelt thanks to my Publicist, for bringing (and continuing to bring) media visibility to *FROM DRIFT to SHIFT*, and sincere gratitude to everyone who provided quotes, insight, and feedback.

I am beholden to every bookstore that has ordered many copies of *FROM DRIFT to SHIFT* and to all platforms who carry it worldwide.

Thank you also to the many companies, organizations and institutions who have invited me to speak about *FROM DRIFT to SHIFT* to their employees, students, members and clients.

I also value and am grateful to leading publications such as *The Huffington Post*˜ and *LinkedIn Pulse*˜ that have enabled me to spread the messages in *FROM DRIFT to SHIFT* so that more readers can benefit.

Thank you to my personal network of friends, family and colleagues who have been there for me throughout the many iterations of this book, numerous meetings, conference calls, and demands on my time. I appreciate their patience, faith, and support as I navigated my way.

And to my inner circle of manuscript reviewers whose honest feedback and enthusiasm kept me going—thank you!

I offer my deepest thanks to you, the reader, for joining me on this quest and for considering the road maps offered in *FROM DRIFT to SHIFT*.

I encourage you today, tomorrow, next month, next year, and for the rest of your life to stay the course. Forge ahead, regardless of what is thrown in your way. Our work permeates our lives. You need the work you are meant to do and the life you are meant to lead to be in sync. This book shows you ways to do that through shifting your perspective, trusting your voice, and taking action.

My hope is that the strategies and stories in this book will assist you in your own life shift, so that you find true happiness in everything you do and in the person you were always meant to be.

Thank you.

INTRODUCTION

"We all love stories. We're born for them. Stories affirm who we are. We all want affirmations that our lives have meaning. And nothing does a greater affirmation than when we connect through stories."
—**Andrew Stanton**, writer of *Toy Story*, TED February 2012

Imagine that you were on your morning commute and you couldn't wait to get to work. You didn't even think of it as work, because you loved it so much.

Imagine you were in a relationship that you only dreamed of in fairytales, and you knew with certainty that it would last forever.

Some of us enjoy these experiences already, while others of us have to wake up and face reality. We're just not there yet.

We all desire to be happy in our work and in our personal lives. Yet, according to a recent Gallup Poll, at least a third of us are not. Why is that?

We spend more than 30 percent of our lives doing something we hate, or we stay in relationships that make us miserable. We just drift along. This statistic bothers me so much. It just doesn't resonate.

So I set out to discover why.

Why do we stay in professional and personal situations that we loathe?

- Is it a fear of risking the unknown?
- Is it a refusal to follow our hearts?
- Is it a need for security?
- Is it a lack of self-esteem?

We all want to be valued for who we are and what we contribute to the world, but when we don't feel useful or worthy in work and life, we spiral downward.

How do we rise up from the pit of despair?

While being stuck can be a conundrum, we are equally perplexed by the people who *have* found true meaning in their work and in their personal lives—people who have found their authenticity, their truth, and are happy, regardless of money, title or power. We admire them.

How do *they* do it? Are they really that different from you and me? I don't think so.

After more than 12 years as a professional Job/Life Coach and Executive Recruiter and after helping thousands of people just like you find true meaning in work and life, I believe I have discovered the roadmap that can get you there—to that place in your life where you are meant to be—so that you too can experience true happiness and fulfillment every day.

Everyone has a story to tell.

We are each born with a unique offering to contribute to the betterment of the world. Some stories stop in their tracks and never move forward. Other stories flow seamlessly (although those are rare from my perspective).

The most engaging stories are those that experience a *shift* somewhere along the way; a shift that gives them the strength, courage, and fortitude to move outside of comfort zones and into places of belonging. These stories overcome, they move upward and onward. They prevail.

These are the stories that motivate, inspire, and give us hope.

I carefully selected the stories in this book to demonstrate that you can overcome anything and achieve a sense of bliss in your own professional and personal life—just like the people you will read about.

In *FROM DRIFT to SHIFT*, you will get the information, insight, and inspiration that you need to find meaning, fulfillment, and happiness in your work and in your life. This is my promise to you.

I want you to be happy, in all things, every day of your life. This is what you deserve—it is your birthright.

When you were born, you had no hang-ups, no fears. All you had was curiosity. You were happy. Why wouldn't you be? All you had to do was watch and absorb.

And then you acted. You acted with abandon, regardless of consequence.

But then something happened along the way that undid that perfect nature you were born with.

I want you to discover your direction so that you can find your happiness. I want you to discover what moves you and to identify the shift you may need to take in your own life in order to achieve success, happiness, and a joy that only comes from doing what you are meant to do and in being who you are truly meant to be.

Between you and me, I have a hunch that you may already know, deep down, what that is. But now it's time to dig deep, see it clearly, and go for it. You only have to answer to *you* in the end. Isn't it time you asked yourself the right questions that will help get you there?

———◆———

In *FROM DRIFT to SHIFT,* you will learn how to ask yourself the right questions and to recognize the opportunity to pursue your true purpose both professionally and personally. When you do, you will find profound success, down to the core of your soul. It is achievable for you, me, and everyone.

FROM DRIFT to SHIFT encourages you to seek a life of meaning; to be curious about who you are and have the courage to hunt for the answers that will help you become the person you are meant to be. Do not let external forces pressure you into being anything less than spectacular.

FROM DRIFT to SHIFT helps you discover how you can make uniquely important contributions to the world.

FROM DRIFT to SHIFT challenges you:

- Why are you in your current job and not in the career of your dreams?
- Are you in the right relationship or are you settling your life away?
- Would you give up your current path to follow that itching voice in your head that says; "Do what you love until you die"?

The people in this book have asked themselves honest and heartfelt questions, and have mustered the courage to make changes so that they can finally live lives of true meaning and happiness. Some have suffered challenges, failures and loss, but they have ultimately triumphed and are living vibrant lives.

They show us firsthand how...

We can let life happen to us or we can make life happen for us.

I want to share a personal story that helped start my own shift.

My great grandmother brought over a box of fancy dishes from Sweden in the early 1900s when she and her husband migrated to the United States. She gave them to my grandmother, who passed them on to my mother. Neither my great grandmother, grandmother, nor mother ever used them...and now they were mine.

"You can't eat off of them," my mother said when she handed over the carton, thick with dust. "They probably have lead in them."

"Seriously?" I replied. "Why did you keep them?"

She looked away. I saw moisture gather in the corners of her eyes, and her hand absently wipe the tears. Then she turned back to me.

"I have no idea. But they are yours now. You should save them."

I slit open the dusty seam of the forgotten box and pulled out a rose-covered plate that had faded with time. I set it in my display cabinet where heirlooms wait to die. I didn't use the plate; after all, it might have lead in it. The rest of the dishes stayed in the box and were placed under the house, where darkness encased them.

Years later, I went through a divorce. As part of purging certain aspects of my old life, I told my mom that it was time to throw out great grandma's dishes. They were still under the house—all but the one plate.

"No!" she exclaimed. "You can't throw out great grandma's dishes. They are our history. They are family."

Really? I thought. *Is this what we do with things that we're supposed to care about—our heirlooms, our money, our jobs, our relationships? Store them away, unexplored, unused, unappreciated, until the time, if at all, when we might actually want to embrace them?*

I didn't believe that was the way to live, yet I was behaving exactly as the women who'd come before me. I was tucking my life away without really living it. How was I any different than great grandma's dishes?

Despite my mother's objection, I knew it was time to throw out those dishes. I was starting a new life; one that I wanted to learn to live as me and not what everyone else expected me to be. If I kept them, it would be like dragging around memories of lives unlived, just to say they existed. It no longer made sense to me.

So I tossed them, one by one, into the colossal dumpster in front of my house—the house where I raised my family, and was now preparing to sell.

As I listened to each delicate cup, saucer, and salad plate dash against the thick steel box, parts of me that had been shattered over the years were released, and I was able to ask myself some honest questions.

- *When was the last time I really felt alive?*
  - When I completed the San Francisco Marathon? When I went on Mr. Toad's Wild Ride at Disneyland with my adult disabled son? When I spent a few days in total silence at a monastery overlooking Big Sur?
- *When was I the truest to myself?*
  - When I left my marriage? When I left investment banking to pursue a more flexible work/life balance? When I finally sat down to write my first novel? When I started going to meditation to learn how to calm my heart?
- *When was I the happiest?*
  - When I played hide-and-seek as a child with the kids in my neighborhood? When I voyaged through Europe with a friend the summer after college? When my own children were born?
- *When did I last feel truly loved?*
  - When I received flowers from a close friend for no reason? When I hosted a dinner with three girlfriends where we told all of our secrets, regardless of the depth of our mistakes? When I received a heartfelt card from my daughter on Mother's Day and had a long, meaningful conversation about life with my son?

I wanted to capture all of those moments, those blissful feelings, and find a way to experience authentic success and happiness on a daily basis.

In this book, you will receive a roadmap through stories about throwing out great grandma's dishes. These are tales about discarding the expectations that bind us and hold us back from living life as our true selves, both in our work and in our relationships.

My hope is that in reading these stories, you will find answers to the most honest questions you can ask about your own work and life.

P.S. I still have the one rose-colored plate. Yes, it's faded, and it may have lead in it, but I use it now and I don't mind it reminding me of where I came from... now that I have clarity.

This book was written with compassion and hope. The stories are written in an accessible style that avoids jargon. They speak openly and directly to the heart.

FROM DRIFT to SHIFT confirms what we all intuitively know, but too often forget: when we realize our place in the world and reach for our highest ideal, amazing things can happen.

PART ONE

WHY SHIFT?

> *"You see the old way wasn't working,*
> *so it's on us to do what we gotta do to survive."*
> **—Tupac Shakur**

Shift

　: to make a change

　: to change or to cause (something or someone) to change to a different opinion, belief, etc.

E verything seems to be going along according to plan, right?

Or not.

You make enough money to support yourself and those you care for, or you have never had enough money. You own a mode of transportation, or you take the bus. You have a house to call your own, or you have rented your whole life. Possibly you've started saving for retirement, or you can barely get by month-to-month. You have a few (or several) close friends, and you are in a relationship. Then again, relationships may not be your thing, and when it comes to friends, well, sometimes they are just not there for you.

Is it a problem if this is what you are used to?

Only you can answer that—and answer you should, because if you dig down deep and are completely honest with yourself, you know that something is missing. If you can relate, I ask you:

Will you be like the masses and do nothing about it? Just go on with your life, saying, It's fine, it's just fine. Or will you bet it all on black, go blindly into the darkness and seek a more fulfilling existence, regardless of the payoff?

According to a Harvard research study, people don't make changes, don't improve their health, relationships, or professional lives. Why? Because they are used to habit. Good or bad, it is hard to change a habit.

Dr. Maxwell Maltz wrote in his book, *Psycho-Cybernetics, A New Way to Get More Living Out of Life* (first published by Prentice Hall in 1960) that it takes 21 days to change a habit. He studied amputees and noticed that it took them 21 days to adapt to the loss of a limb, and concluded that this hypothesis applied to any major life change.

I'm not sure Andy Wirth, CEO of Squaw Valley Ski Resort Holdings, would agree with Dr. Maltz. Andy basically lost his arm, nothing left but raw bone; and while it was reconstructed piece by piece, he has still not fully adapted to the reconfigured limb. He has had 25 operations to prove it.

Life has to be more than habit or settling for your current situation.

You are unique and are meant to do amazing things. You were not put here to go through life like a routine, with no emotional charge, with fear to hold you back and security (or lack of it) to handcuff you. It may be time for you to change your habits and shift your life in the direction that brings you to a place where you get up every day pumped for what lies ahead.

LET'S GET DOWN TO THE NITTY GRITTY

- Are you unhappy in your job?
- Are you just drifting along?
- Are you doing what you have always dreamed of doing?
- Are you with the love of your life?
- Are you with someone for safety and security?
- Do you wish you could travel to the corners of the earth but come up with reasons why you never go?
- Do you have a secret passion that you have never pursued?
- Do you hate getting out of bed in the morning?

If you have answered yes to even one of these questions, and no to some real important ones, it's time for you to make a shift in your life. That shift may happen to you and wake you up to life. It may happen for you by the stars lining up just so, or you may actually initiate it. Whichever way it comes, it may be time—that is, if you really want to live a full, happy life.

I frequent a local restaurant where I grab a salad at lunchtime, and have gotten to know the gal who always seems to be on duty. We struck up a conversation the other day.

"Are you in college here?" I asked.

"I'm working off my student loans." She seemed okay with her situation and had a cheery disposition.

"So you like your job?"

Her dimples disappeared. "It's okay. It's not really what I want to do though."

"Really? What *do* you want to do?"

"You'll think it's silly."

I laughed out loud. She had no idea I was writing a book about finding meaning in work and in life. "Actually, I am interested. What is it that you *really* want to do?"

I could see her thoughts racing. *Should I tell her my real dream or the one she wants to hear. Should I tell her I want to join a start-up, become a banker or a lawyer?*

Her shoulders relaxed and the dimples reappeared—and then she leaned across the counter that separated us. I felt as though I was about to be let in on a great secret.

"I want to own a bakery."

How perfect. She looked like the owner of a bakery to me right away. Why? Because it was what her heart desired, and it flooded across her face.

"But there aren't any in this town. I mean, Starbucks has some stuff they sell, but no real bakery."

I wanted to help. "Have you ever heard of Rustic Bakery? It's big in the Bay Area."

Her pale blue eyes widened and her cropped blond hair bounced. "No, I haven't."

"Well, in my opinion, they make the best croissants I've ever had. They have every kind of amazing pastry you could want, plus flatbread crackers that Whole Foods now carries. The best part is it's all organic."

"Wow. That sounds great. I should look into them."

"Yes. You should call them and see if you can be an apprentice. That's what you should do." I hoped I didn't overstep my bounds, but I really wanted to see this sweet gal follow her dream.

Her smile turned into a grin.

Will she do it? Will she risk it all, call Rustic Bakery, work for free, bake out of her kitchen, whatever it takes? Or will she continue to waitress at the local salad place, work off her student loans, meet a guy, get married, have babies and call it a day? Not that any of that is bad, but I want to see her have a life that she is really living, with all its experiences, its ups and downs, challenges and triumphs—not a life that is *just fine*.

———◆———

What about you? Would you put it all on the line for your dream?

I urge you to read on and see how others have made significant shifts in their lives that have led them to live lives of exuberance, passion, purpose, and fulfillment.

When we make a shift, we see the world more clearly. We go from a tumultuous wave on the surface to deep water calm. We learn to value joy, passion, and a sense of fulfillment that transcends money, power, status, and stuff.

Chapter 1

SHIFT HAPPENS

Serita and Reid Cox – Co-Founders of iFoster

I recently watched *Birdman*, the 2015 Academy Award-winning film for Best Picture. Michael Keaton (who plays an actor trying to reinvent himself), and his nemesis played by Ed Norton were stellar. But it was what Emma Stone said (who plays Keaton's rehabbed daughter and theatre assistant), that stayed with me long after the movie ended. Her short, angry tirade at her father, when he discovers that she is still doing drugs, is the underlying theme of this chapter.

She says, "You are only doing this play because you want to be relevant. You want to matter. There are people out there every day who want to matter and fight to matter, but they just don't. It sucks. And guess what? No one gives a s***."

When we don't think we are relevant in the world, that we don't matter and that no one cares, we stop trying. When we stop trying, all sorts of bad comes our way.

Meet Serita.

Serita started the first year of life by being taken away from her family and put into the foster care system.

When we sat down to talk about her life, it started simply.

"Where were you born?"

"My birth certificate says Ottawa, Canada." She had no attachment to it.

"I was removed for the sake of my personal safety and, since I was a baby, it's all just a big void. I prefer it that way."

Serita is matter-of-fact and emotionless when it comes to bringing up her painful past, as can often be the case for the neglected. There was nothing good for her there. The biggest impact on her early childhood was that her mother gave her up, leaving Serita to feel unwanted. It wasn't her fault. She didn't ask to be born.

Many of us are brought into this world and placed in situations that we never asked for. It's how we deal with it, in part, that helps shape us into who we are. Will we just go along or will we find a way out? Will we take what's given to us or will we create our own future, our own version of success?

Take someone from the projects. How does he or she get out of the violence, the drugs, the system? Is it education? Not always. Is it an internal drive that can't be snuffed out? Maybe. Whatever it is within you, you must listen to it and not simply accept the cards and expectations that society deals you. You are one of a kind; there is no one like you on the planet and you have gifts to offer yourself and the world.

Serita reminds me of someone who should have lived in the 20s. She has dark, pixie length hair that frames her face as though she slept in pin curls. Her beaded collars and layered skirts make me want to swing dance, and sometimes she wears vintage pants and faded shirts that remind me of workers who built the Golden Gate Bridge. Serita delights in second hand stores and has a vintage presence that makes me smile.

Her home in the mountains is vintage too, with a delightful series of tiny rooms, thick velvet drapes and secret passages. It feels like a salon where you might host a poetry reading or séance. When you visit, you discover all sorts of collections from her travels. A set of tiny metal figurine chess pieces from the Middle East, a gift of African masks and spears, a giant flowing lithograph of a 20s woman in Paris.

Serita surrounds herself with symbols of authenticity, identity, and freedom. She strived for many years to find where she belonged in the world, but it didn't come easy. How could it when you started out faced with forgotten?

———◆———

The foster care system in Canada placed Serita with Dolly, a teacher type who had a full and chaotic daycare center in her home and some grandkids that were part of the day program now and then. Serita was the only child who slept over each night—on the couch.

Dolly was nice, she just had lots of rules, which were needed with so many kids running around. Serita had a roof over her head and a stable environment. That's what Dolly was required to do by Social Services. Tinker the dog is Serita's fondest memory of Dolly's house.

"She was an old black lab that let you hug her, climb on her, and probably even poke her in the eye if you played too aggressively with her."

Serita recalls some snapshots of her during that time, but she doesn't relate to them. Serita is good at compartmentalizing her past.

While the official goal of the foster care system is reunification whenever possible and then alternate permanency in the U.S. system, for Serita: "They just want to get you back with your family—which sucks."

After spending six years at Dolly's, Serita's younger brother was born and she was reunited with her family.

"I was assigned to my home—that's all." But this wasn't any better for her than it was when she was taken away. Her parents still didn't give a crap about her, and she knew it.

Serita was arrested at eight years old. The police officer who cuffed her never did ask why she was trying to steal a sharp weapon. She was simply trying to survive, but no one cared enough to inquire.

As a result, Serita was officially introduced into Canada's dependency and delinquency courts, which would release her on probation. This opened a door to darkness. It would take a paramount shift for her to find her way out.

"Why *don't* people care? Are they too involved with their own importance?" I asked Serita.

"Assumptions are made. No one ever asks. I could either capitulate, turn to self-loathing, or simply say, screw them. I chose the latter."

But what of the kids who don't take the bull by the horns? The ones who let life screw them instead of the other way around? Sometimes you have to be like Serita and decide that you are a survivor.

Are you a survivor?

I grew up in a house with seven people and one bathroom. We had little money. I started making bright colored cardboard bracelets and selling them to the local hippy shop for three bucks each when I was nine. I put on plays and carnivals with the kids on my street and charged a quarter for admission. I never owned a pair of jeans until college. I am a survivor.

As an "at risk" youth, Serita was officially on the juvenile watch list, and while she was sent back home after the incident, from that moment forward, she did all she could to stay away. Serita knew it wasn't ideal at home and that no one was really going to help her, so she would help herself.

"Was your brother safe?"

"A little more than me because my unstable mother wanted a boy—but not really. Screw them."

Serita became really good at couch surfing at friends' homes and, due to the reality of life's basic needs, she started to borrow—clothes, shoes, food, just about anything to fulfill her needs. She did what she had to do.

Serita was happy as long as she wasn't at home.

She was definitely system-affected, so how bad could it get? She only had herself to rely on and took her path into her own hands.

Serita cared deeply for her brother and, although she wasn't home much, she stuck around on the fringes long enough to help raise him. However, as fate would have it, he too became a delinquent.

> **You may be surprised to learn that there are many
> famous people who started out as delinquents.**

Take Mark Wahlberg. According to records, when his parents split, he got involved with the wrong crowd, got into drugs, dropped out of school, and was charged with attempted murder. Now he's one of Hollywood's top paid actors. He is a survivor.

Or take country singer, Merle Haggard. At nine he was fatherless, which led him to seek out his own guidance, landing him in juvenile detention for stealing a 13mm gun. A year later, he was arrested for petty larceny and put in the high security Preston School of Industry. He had a lot of time to think and while there went through his own shift. Merle earned his high school diploma and started making his way to the top of the country music scene.

Sometimes we regret what we do to survive, and sometimes we just have to do what we do to survive. And it's not always because of being from a broken family like Serita, Mark, Merle, or me. I am privy to plenty of very wealthy kids from prominent families who are drug abusers, suicidal, and self-loathers. Conditions cross all socio-economic borders. It's recognizing our situation and the fact that we need to make a shift; and then figuring out how we do it, that makes or breaks us.

Serita attended an alternative cross-boundary high school called Glebe in Ottawa that straddles a socioeconomically diverse community. Glebe is for kids with all sorts of situations and who are from all walks of life. The school accepts everyone, which makes it kind of cool.

Some need independent study (like actor Tom Cruise (before her time there) and singer Alanis Morissette), because they have blossoming careers and require flexible schedules. Other kids have families who travel a lot. Some kids are rich and others very poor. Some youths are hooked on drugs, can't handle the rigor of a normal high school, or are delinquents like Serita.

"I got kicked out the first week of high school because I skipped. We didn't have lockers because they didn't want us storing anything. The school was way over crowded; built for 2,500 but taught 5,000. We weren't allowed to congregate in public, so I never got to go to a football game or dance. There was a principal's office, but no one ever got sent there because the line would be too long."

"It must have been challenging."

"We were just a bunch of hooligans. Every day at noon someone would pull the fire alarm. It would take at least two hours to get everyone out of the building and back to class. Most of us left for the rest of the day. We were usually drunk by then anyway, so what was the point? After several weeks of the daily fire alarm, the fire department stopped coming over. Kids did drugs in the bathrooms sometimes too, which led to teachers patrolling the hallways and the police coming by. S*** happens."

———◆———

But despite all the presumed chaos, Serita loved Glebe. She loved the diversity and the fun. The teaching was excellent.

"I learned a lot there. A lot academically, and about life."

Glebe is also the high school for kids trying to get permanent residency. Canada is a pretty welcoming country and the school is bustling with people from around the world.

"At the time, there was one group considered the Vietnamese boat people. They were the Asian contingent. They resided mostly on the second floor, middle hallway. None of them spoke English, but they did cook their meals in the hallways. It always smelled good down there. The Haitians ruled the basement and the druggies who did stuff like shrooms and LSD, hung out in the bathrooms. There was a group called GBs and they basically kept watch. My high school was like the United Nations. I met people from all over the world, which was cool, along with a bunch of renegades like me."

"Did you play any sports—or maybe you weren't there enough to?"

"Yeah. I played water polo and flag football, so I was pretty strong and fast. If anyone messed with me, I could move quickly so that I didn't get hurt. Like the time our team got kicked out of the league for beating up the opposing flag football team before the game. They were making fun of us, so we basically defended our honor and moved fast enough to get the better of them. I didn't get to play that sport after that.

We didn't beat anyone up in water polo though, at least not on the surface. Under water was another story. Sometimes I had to stick up for myself and my team."

While some might conclude that Serita could be misconstrued as an angry kid because of all she had been through; she likes to focus on the fact that her high school was actually fun in a weird, dysfunctional way. She got along and made many friends who became like family. It was home life that she avoided.

According to Biographer Walter Isaacson, there was the "Good Steve (Jobs)," and then, there was the "Bad Steve." Even some of the most successful people in the world seemed to experience apparent bouts of anger or discontent at various points in their lives. When Jobs went to college, he didn't even say goodbye when his adoptive parents dropped him off.

Jobs' reasoning: "I didn't want anyone to know I had parents. I wanted to be like an orphan who had bummed around the country on trains and just arrived out of nowhere, with no roots, no connections, no background." Would you say Steve was an angry kid—or maybe just drifting?

Serita realized something else during high school, which was the beginning of her journey toward self-awareness. There were actually people who cared.

"I developed a sort of family with the girls on the water polo team. I think it helped me."

Several of Serita's teammates knew of her plight. Rather than embarrass her because she basically had no home, couldn't afford clothes, and had to walk everywhere (regardless of the weather or time), they came up with an idea. Everyone would share clothes. *Team Share* was the nicest thing anyone had ever done for Serita, even though they made it appear as though it was for everyone. She was grateful.

Serita went on to play water polo for Junior Team Canada, which was a very high level accomplishment and a highlight of her childhood.

> *"Because of my team and some big successes,*
> *I became more tolerant and accepting of others."*

Having someone who cares and lets you know that you matter (like Serita's teammates) or having a mentor early in your life or career, can make all the difference in the world.

———◆———

Serita was a competitive runner in middle school but broke her back at 14. Rehab became swimming, which is how she became a water polo player in the first place.

"It was more fun than swimming laps."

"Did your brother go to Glebe?"

"He went to a Jesuit high school for delinquents—only boys. It was better for him. I am very proud of my brother. He didn't have it as hard as me, but it was still hard. He graduated and got into the Navy—well sort of. Once they found out that he had a felony record, he was rejected. He became a really good commercial diver instead."

The smile returned to her face. Serita loves her brother deeply.

"Did you ever want to have a super power?"

"My brother and I used to pretend we could be flies on the wall—we were invisible and could sneak into places and see what was going on."

I thought this super power fit Serita perfectly. It's important to be aware of your environment, and Serita's environment during her formative years made her very aware, which also taught her to be well prepared for anything.

"What were the academics like in your school?"

This might have been the biggest break Serita could have gotten and was the most important shift for her, yet.

"I figured that they had to give someone an 'A' in each class, so why not me? School was pretty easy, so I applied myself."

"So you did well?"

"Well, I skipped class a lot, but I did start getting A's. I figured the odds were in my favor because no one else cared if they got good grades. I also knew that I was going to go to college like everyone does in Canada, so I might as well go for the grades to increase my options."

Serita started to figure things out, but it was usually on her own. She wasn't as concerned about having adults care about her, they hadn't anyway, but approval and acceptance by her peers was important to her.

"Like most youth in foster care, it's not about the adults. You don't trust adults so you don't seek caring."

Then something amazing happened.
Serita had a Physics Teacher who believed in her.

"The sad thing is, the guy changed my life, but I can't remember his name."

Serita does recall her Chemistry teacher's name though. She felt embarrassed when, after she hadn't done her homework, he called her out in front of the class and told her that if she went to University, it would be a waste of everyone's time and hard earned money.

"Why is it that I can recall all the bad stuff from my life, but I feel so guilty that I can't remember all the good?"

———◆———

During her senior year, Serita walked into her Physics class and *no name teacher* told her that she needed to take the Waterloo Physics Exam (an international competition)—now. Only a couple of people who did well on the test got scholarship money for university, and he thought she just might.

"I was so pissed off. I had to sit down right then, without any prep work offered, and take a waste-of-my-time exam. I was planning on an athletic scholarship anyway. I didn't have any money."

Serita scored in the top 10% worldwide.

———◆———

Why do we sabotage ourselves into believing that we don't deserve anything good in life?

Is it our upbringing, our fear of the unknown, or do we resign ourselves to failure because maybe it's just easier that way? According to a 2012 *Forbes* article by David DeSalvo on failure, it's what we believe and what we are told that holds us down.

———◆———

In the Canadian system you are allowed to pick three schools to have your transcripts sent to for free. Serita applied to Ottawa, Carleton College and Queens University. She got into all of them.

She had won a National Science and Engineering Scholarship that is a Canadian scholarship good at any school so long as the emphasis was science or engineering.

Serita chose Carleton College where she majored in Aerospace Engineering.

———◆———

After college, Serita didn't want to go home, so she went straight to graduate school.

She applied to Harvard, MIT, and McGill University (the Harvard of Canada) and was accepted to all three. Serita decided to attend McGill on a full ride.

While she dreamed of majoring in journalism, she was really good at science and math, so she became a biochemistry and biotechnology major.

All of a sudden, something inside Serita clicked. She had her ticket out, a real chance to matter. Maybe it was time to let it all go and get rid of that chip on her shoulder, even if it wasn't her fault.

Shift.

———————◆———————

Meet Reid.

Reid grew up poor in a small town in Canada where farmers were the elite and everyone else was white trash.

"You may not think of farmers as elite, but in my town, they were royalty. I was not. Even though we owned the local marina, I grew up with no money. It was all I knew, so money has never held a big role in my life."

Reid was educated in a two-room schoolhouse with three grades in each class. "It was as close to poverty without being homeless as you can get."

Reid is mellow and witty and accepting of whatever life brings his way. He doesn't seem to get too worked up about anything—but I can tell there is passion in him, even if it appears dormant.

His fair skin and close shaven head fits him perfectly. Nothing fancy. Whatever. It doesn't really matter to him. He is a day-to-day kind of guy.

Because Reid grew up poor and neither of his parents went to college, there were no expectations put on him. This can be very freeing for a kid, although he didn't realize it at the time.

———————◆———————

In today's world, competition is so fierce. Parents swirl around their kids, whom they stick in the eye of the pressure storm: do well in school, be the best at your sport, instrument, or art. If you sing, get on **American Idol.**

If you dance, the professional ballet route could be profitable
—for goodness sakes, at least get a trophy!

Bragging rights are big in our society, but for Reid, there was nothing to brag about.

Reid ended up doing well in school, despite the cramped quarters and opted to attend university because the government basically paid for it, so why not? His sister went, too. His parents didn't care either way. No pressure.

He chose the University of Western Ontario and majored in Organizational Psychology because he was curious as to why people did what they did and wanted to understand why some treated others differently because of status. It was silly and interesting at the same time. He let the wind guide him and had no family legacy to follow, so he just immersed himself and did well.

After university, he took a year off to travel and play volleyball in Australia. It sounded like fun, so off he went once again.

As time lingered on, Reid realized that he would have to get a job at some point and figured that people who went to business school got jobs, so he applied to McGill and got in.

That's where he met Serita.

"She was so vivacious, attractive, and outgoing. I was quieter."

McGill was very international, so they were always going out with people from all over the world. They gained perspective. The curriculum was hard, but not grueling, so they both did well again while also having time to enjoy new and interesting friends.

Serita and Reid had a lot in common. They both came from no money and so they didn't really care about it. Each had jobs during their master's programs, which helped with expenses. They did what they had to do to get through. They didn't let ego guide them. This approach set them up for the future.

If they ever bet on something and lost it all, they would just figure out
a way to make it back. There was no safety net.

Serita forged ahead with energy and dedication to whatever she faced. Her "screw them" approach drove her forward and never back.

Reid became a good planner, methodical, and didn't live in fear. When you've been at the bottom, what is there to be afraid of? He learned how to budget and manage his time. In a weird way, Reid felt in control of his life.

Together they started to listen to their hearts instead of the expectations of society. Serita began talking about wanting to help kids.

———◆———

"Do you consider yourself a risk taker?" I asked Reid.

"I am a risk taker *and* I am risk adverse. How's that for methodical? If I think something can be pulled off, I will risk; so it's within the context of measured belief as opposed to blind passion."

"You and Serita never had kids."

"That's right. We figured that if we could help hundreds or even thousands of kids versus having just one, that might be the better way to go." And so they continued to talk now and then about Serita's passion: the foster care system.

Reid believes that Serita is the smarter of the two. She is four years younger and graduated a year before him from McGill. Serita is quick to remind that Reid got a percentage point higher on the GMATs. Ninety-ninth percentile. I would say they are both pretty brilliant.

Serita wanted to go into strategic consulting, so she joined Deloitte and, eventually, moved over to Bain & Company.

Reid took a job in investment research with Toronto Dominion Bank and then Deacon Capital. He was in the gold mining space and liked the hands-on approach of visiting the mines and understanding the geological dynamics. Reid spent a lot of time invisible and underground, not unlike growing up in a town where non-farmers were treated much the same.

Investment Banking Research Analysts used to not have to go down into the mines, but years earlier, Bre-X Minerals, the largest Canadian gold mining entity, changed the way things were done. They grew from $0 to $6 billion in cash practically overnight—but there was never any gold. The entire operation was a sham and temporarily crushed the industry. After that, checks and balances got stringent.

As a Research Analyst, Reid had to validate recommendations made on behalf of his employers and, luckily for them, he didn't mind going deep and climbing down the shafts. Someone had to do it to make sure another Bre-X didn't happen.

"I identified with the hard lives the workers lived, and the fact that they had little to show for it."

———◖———

One night Serita and Reid were out for dinner and decided to write down the three cities in the world where they would like to live. San Francisco matched and so the next week, a fortuitous transfer opened up at Bain Consulting and Serita took it.

Reid followed Serita to San Francisco a few months later, after he wrapped up his final job in Canada at Lowen Ondaatje McCutcheon Ltd. He was hoping to land at another investment bank, but the market was in turmoil and there were thousands of unemployed finance guys vying for similar roles. Being the laid back guy Reid is, he figured that he would be fine; after all, when you come from nothing, there's really nothing to lose. He had faith that something would come up, and it did.

Reid joined Pac-West Telecomm as a Corporate Officer in investor relations and Business Development. But Pac-West eventually went under and Reid moved over to consulting in investor relations for companies wanting to grow and/or go public.

Serita ended up joining 3Com, a major client of Bain, and was instrumental in the dividing up of the company.

———◖———

It's important to look for the signs when you are wondering if you should make a shift. They are there and you need to be observant.

Think about it. Maybe you have been considering buying a new Mini Cooper, for example. All of a sudden, every other car you see is a Mini Cooper. Or let's say you want to have a baby. Suddenly everyone is pregnant.

Pay close attention to what you see, and hear, and more importantly, imagine. The capacity of our brains to realize our desires is strong.

According to *Emotional Memory Management: Positive Control Over Your Memory* by Joseph M. Carver, Ph.D., the mind can experience something, even if you don't actually do it. For example: Psychologists at the University of Chicago divided up equally talented basketball players into three groups. Group one practiced hoop shots every day for a month. Group two imagined making the shots, but never actually threw the ball. Group three, the control group, did nothing. Guess what happened? When it came time to test the talent, Group two never missed, without ever practicing even one throw.

———◆———

Your mind is a powerful machine; use it to your advantage and when you are ready to make a shift, the signs will appear. Follow your instincts, focus on what you want and just jump in. If you spend too much time ignoring the signs and simply preparing because you are afraid, you may never make the change that you so deeply need to lead a fulfilling life.

———◆———

Reid enjoyed investor relations consulting and ended up catching a favorable blow of the wind, which landed him at LinkedIn™. He ended up being part of the team that helped take the company public.

Social media was a pretty new concept then (people still weren't too sure what Facebook and Twitter were) and the dot com bubble had burst. Investors and the market were skittish, but LinkedIn, an aggregated community of business professionals, aimed at revenue generation from recruiters, was a home run.

For Serita, 3Com was divided and done and she wasn't loving her work as much. She had just riffed (fired) over 10,000 people and that didn't feel too good.

At 27 years old, Serita had already accomplished her goal of being a Senior Executive in a Fortune 500 Company.

Serita's desire to help the in-between kids in foster care continued to nag at her. She became intrigued with The Bridgespan Group; Bain's non-profit consulting arm.

"It would be pretty arrogant of me to think that I could just start a non-profit. I wanted to do it right, so I set out to learn."

Serita moved over to Bridgespan with the intent of learning how to start and successfully run a non-profit. She made it clear to Bridgespan from the beginning that she was there to learn and eventually form a non-profit that bridged the gap between child welfare and the juvenile justice system. She was not interested in becoming a partner and they were happy to have her on board.

Serita was on her way to making her biggest shift yet—the one she was always meant to make.

The signs added up.

- Her high school physics teacher had faith in her by making her take the test, which she scored off the charts on, and which opened the door for her to a top business school.
- She did well in corporate America, all the while knowing that she wanted to help kids like her who had been forgotten.
- She paid attention to the signs:
  - The transfer to SF that came up when she and Reid wrote down their favorite cities on a napkin.
  - The opportunity at Deloitte, Bain, and 3Com.
  - The move to Bridgespan that enabled her to learn how to run a non-profit properly; including recruiting a board, understanding government politics, and how to operate such an entity.
  - The money she was able to make to actually self-fund the starting phase of a non-profit.

For Reid, the signs lined up too.

He and Serita had a lot in common and both wanted to make a difference for the less fortunate; and while Reid's passions may not have lain in helping non-farmers or the guys who risked their lives going down into the gold and diamond mines (although he cared very much for these communities), he did want to give back and help some neglected group get a leg up.

"Serita had the deep passion and specific vision. She always did. I knew I could be helpful in a CFO-type role, and we thought that with a non-profit, we just might be able to help thousands of kids. It was a pretty lofty goal, but exciting too. So iFoster was born."

"Did you know how to start it?"

"Not really and sort of. We kind of took from our experience and jumped in. If we spent too much more time preparing, we may never have done it. Serita learned a lot about operations while at Bridgespan and I knew a lot about finance. And we both had experience with all of this free stuff that came with corporate incentive plans that were part of both of our employment. Why not buy one of those plans for foster kids and families and anyone in the system to access?"

"How did you get it?"

"We bet the ranch. We leveraged everything. We both knew what it was like to lose everything, so we didn't really care if we did. We decided to go for it."

So Serita and Reid set out to aggregate a community, not unlike Facebook or LinkedIn, but for the foster care community sector. With the corporate plan, they had the ability to provide everything for the foster care system: rides, childcare, coupons, meals, housing, whatever was needed. And the participants didn't have to go through government paperwork or long waits to get what they needed.

They didn't have a Board of Directors or any other source of funding, only their savings and their house. They put it all on the line.

Serita remembered the weekend they were heading out of town on a short vacation; right after she had created a very simple community website and had sent out a bunch of emails to government and foster agencies across the country. She had asked for their input on the idea of a non-profit like iFoster that would bridge the gap between the public system and the needs of the outside world. By the time they returned a few days later, they had so many replies and registrations, they were blown away.

Reid and Serita were onto something viable.

"The State of Georgia was first to reply and the State of New York really put us on the map. They sent our idea out to all of their agencies. The response was huge."

I could see by the smile on Serita's face that she and Reid were at the beginning of the realization of their dream.

"iFoster is like a witness protection plan for foster," Reid continued during one of our visits. "For example, children are removed from their home environments and placed in safe places, but are fragmented due to their privacy and security needs."

"We applied the principles of the internet and social media to aggregate an unconnected community with many facets: agencies, foster kids, foster families, resources..."

"How do you vet the community?"

"It can be anonymous, although we have checks and balances to make sure they are legitimate. We can't invade their privacy. HIPAA rights and all."

"What exactly does iFoster do and what part of the system does it serve?"

Reid and Serita both explained how iFoster helps kids in the system, with the sweet spot for real impact being the ages 16-26. These are the real in-between kids. They weren't adopted when they were cute babies, and they will soon age out of the government system when they turn 18. They truly are the forgotten.

iFoster helps foster kids get what they need to survive and thrive, with money from private sources.

The non-profit helps the kids prepare for and get jobs too. For example, iFoster partners with Starbucks and large grocery chains that have agreed to consider iFoster's trained kids first for any job openings that fit. They have an impressive hiring success rate, but the kids have to go through an intensive boot camp of training and interview prep first. If they pass, they are sent out for consideration. If not, they can always come back and try again.

Recently, iFoster and Starbucks put on a holiday campaign where every kid up to age 20, in each county, from Sacramento north, where Starbucks had stores, not only received a holiday gift, but one they actually wanted. Serita and her staff put the little holiday tags on trees and brought them to each store. Customers could pick out a tag, buy the toy and drop it off at any Starbucks. The toys were sorted and distributed by the case workers.

There were 173 stores, 7,000 presents. The government can't accept gifts on behalf of foster kids through companies like Starbucks, but they can through iFoster.

"Everyone had so much fun with this effort, from iFoster to the agencies to Starbucks employees, and it is going to be even bigger next year. We need to hire more people!" Serita laughed.

Another cool thing about iFoster is that they only hire people who have their stories; people who have experienced foster care or some sort of complex childhood that gives them the passion needed to dedicate endless hours to a cause that is often unrecognized. But in their hearts, they are full.

I ended my visits with a few questions:

"Do you think you'll ever have kids or maybe foster one?"

Reid: "We have always thought about fostering, and it is not out of the question. If we did, it would likely be a teenager, right in our target group, because a teen would have a blast in the mountains where we live."

Serita was in complete agreement.

"What is the most important thing in the world to you?"

"Reid. And helping foster kids."

"Serita. And helping foster kids."

Serita and Reid found passion, each other, purpose, and meaning in their work and in their lives. It was a long, hard road for both, then it was easier, and finally they risked it all for what they believed in. In their case, they succeeded and their agency seems to be growing every year.

What's the ultimate goal of iFoster?

"That all children growing up outside of their biological homes have the resources and opportunities to achieve their full potential."

iFoster was recently recognized by the California Assembly and this was read into the record by Congresswoman Doris Matsui on April 29, 2016:

In Recognition of iFoster

Mr. Speaker, I rise today to honor the iFoster jobs program for foster youth.

Each May, we recognize National Foster Care Month, when we acknowledge the unique challenges facing American youth in foster care. The campaign recognizes not only the foster youth, but also the foster parents, family members, child welfare professionals, volunteers, and members of our communities who help our children find foster placements, and ultimately transition successfully out of the foster care system. One of the most significant challenges facing foster youth as they transition out of the foster care system involves finding meaningful employment.

As a Member of the Congressional Caucus on Foster Youth, I am committed to identifying strategies to improve the well-being, education, and employment outcomes for our foster youth. For these reasons, I ask my colleagues to join me in recognizing iFoster's foster youth employment program. The iFoster program was launched in Placer County in May 2015 and has since expanded to Los Angeles County. Through a partnership with the grocery industry, it has developed an innovative employment program for transition age foster youth.

The program provides participating youth with pre-employment skills training, employer matching, needed material resources, preferential hiring, on-the-job mentorship, and scholarship and career advancement activities. In its pilot year, the program has placed over 100 youth, and achieved a 100 percent hire rate and a 90 percent six-month retention rate for participating foster youth. I am pleased that this May, the program will be launching in Riverside, San Bernardino, and Sacramento counties, before being replicated nationwide. Mr. Speaker, in advance of iFoster's expansion next month, I ask all my colleagues to join me in honoring its work in the State of California.

Chapter 1 Takeaways

- S*** Happens. Deal with it and move forward.
- Lay it on the line and never give up. Ever!
- You matter, even if no one ever tells you that you do.
- Be as positive as you can.
- The harder you had it, the easier your life becomes. You've lived through it, so nothing is too big of a deal.
- Own your story.
- Your ideal job may change over time. If you love what you do as you do it, each phase can be rewarding and the next chapter will naturally unfold.
- When you reach a big goal, set a new one; even if it's in a different direction.
- Don't hate—appreciate.
- No one is as dumb as you want them to be.
- Smile! Laugh and have fun. You only live once.
- Have the curiosity and confidence to go beyond where you are told.
- Many are compensated for doing what they don't love. Do what you love.
- Idea: Let everyone assign $1 of their owed taxes to a non-profit of their choosing.

Chapter 2

AGAINST ALL ODDS

**Emilee Garfield – Cancer Survivor, Movement Educator,
Certified Wellness Coach**

"Cancer saved my life."

E milee is a young, vivacious woman, who is basically raising her children on her own while holding down two demanding jobs as a Movement Educator and Certified Wellness Coach.

"I should have died twice," she said as we sat at her kitchen table and began our conversation. "I used to live in fear; fear of love, dying, relationships, cancer. Now I have no fear. Actually, I don't give a s*** what anyone thinks about me. I have chosen to embrace life. After all, I was given a lot of chances."

She crinkles her sparkling eyes, opens her mouth wide and lets out a laugh that is infectious. It's almost as though she is shocked at her own words, but she goes with it and I instantly want to celebrate with her. I can feel her sense of freedom.

It was clear that Emilee had already shifted when I met her. She can teach about it. And, in a way she already does when she coaches people about their life purpose and encourages them to go after their innermost dreams. Or when she helps cancer survivors recover when they have scars left over from operations that have cut through muscle, leaving no core strength to rely on.

She smiles big and exudes confidence, which gives others the will to live. And in doing so, her inner resolve grows too.

But it wasn't always this way.

At four years old, Emilee was diagnosed with a rare childhood cancer called Rhabdomyosarcoma. Basically, it's a cancer of the connective tissue between the bladder and uterus, including the vagina and the tissues throughout the pelvis.

"When they opened me up, my tumor had grown to the size of a grapefruit, and had metastasized. They told my mom it was inoperable." I watched as droplets filled the base of Emilee's eyes, but she quickly wiped them away.

Two years of radiation and chemotherapy ravaged Emilee's body. Her parents separated.

According to the *Acute Stress in Parents of Children Newly Diagnosed with Cancer* published on the National Center for Biotechnology Information website, after studying close to 200 families, the following was concluded:

Immediately following their child's diagnosis of cancer, most mothers and fathers experience SAS (Symptoms of Acute Stress), with a subsample meeting criteria for ASD (Acute Stress Disorder). More anxious parents are at heightened risk of more intense reactions. The findings support the need for evidence-based psychosocial support at diagnosis and throughout treatment for families who are at risk for acute distress reactions.

Stress was high in Emilee's family. Her mother increased her workload to three jobs in order to pay for the treatments. She showed up for her daughter even though she too could have crumbled.

Unfortunately, Emilee's father ended his own life soon thereafter.

"He served in Vietnam and had been affected with PTSD due to Agent Orange. Then, I got cancer. Maybe it was all too much for him."

Emilee was not told about the true nature of her father's death until high school. She always thought it was due to a hunting accident. Maybe this was good for her because she had to find strength to fight a cancer that was eating away at her from the inside out.

Somehow, someway, Emilee survived. She was given the first of several new chances at life.

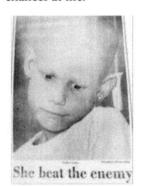

She beat the enemy

Emilee with cancer at a very young age.

Still, life was hard, even beyond beating cancer.

Because Emilee's mom was working around the clock, Emilee was often left home alone to bear the pain and loneliness of the disease. When out in public with her mom, she had to endure the stares of strangers and, on a deeper level, the alienation of friends.

We all want so much to feel connected, loved, and know that we matter. If we start out in life not feeling these important elements due to environmental conditions or those beyond our control, such as cancer, imagine how these feelings can permeate all areas of life as we age. Our relationships, careers and emotional state can all be affected.

An article in *The Telegraph* claims that careers can suffer when a person has experienced a childhood disease. The article goes on to say that those who are either born with a low birth weight or spend at least four weeks in the hospital as a child, tend to be promoted less in the workplace.

While the study looked at 8,300 people in a particular industry and whose lives were followed for 13 years, it states that this does not necessarily apply to every sector or socioeconomic level. However, it does point to less advancement in the workplace in general.

KidsHealth.org discusses the element of childhood self-esteem as armor against the challenges of the world. But when you don't have it due to the alienation you experience from a disease; then what? According to KidsHealth, all sorts of emotional problems can ensue, not even taking into consideration the strain of surviving the disease or the nagging possibility that it may return.

Emilee doesn't have much recollection of kindergarten through 5th grade, but she does remember going to gymnastics and doing her best to keep up a spunky disposition, despite feelings of uncertainty on the inside.

"Being bald and carrying a permanent scar that spans from the bottom of my breast at my sternum bone to practically my public bone made me feel shameful and embarrassed. It was a constant reminder." Yet, Emilee knew that she had been given a miraculous chance at life.

She isn't sure how she gathered the resolve at such a young age, but, somehow, even with the cancer and the death of her father, Emilee decided to enter the world rather than hide from it.

As she started her teenage years, Emilee kept her cancer as quiet as possible. She had moved to a new school at the end of 6th grade from one where she had felt alone and embarrassed just for being who she was.

"There were days when I felt quietly worthless. As a kid, this is a terrible feeling. I dreaded PE because I had to change my clothes." Emilee would lock herself in the bathroom stall so that no one could see her scar. Being in a new town was like a brand new life: it gave her the opportunity for people to get to know Emilee, not Cancer Girl.

In high school, Emilee became a cheerleader. Every time the short shirt of her uniform road up her stomach, she pulled it down. She was making friends and becoming popular, which was a great new feeling. Emilee was healing emotionally, but dating scared her. Being touched, even if it was just a hand on her belly, made her cringe. Emilee avoided affection.

"I was afraid to love or be loved. Cancer can do that to someone."

Meanwhile, she still needed surgery to have her scar revised. The operation was akin to reconstructive surgery, which included a vaginoplasty, which is not unlike what a transsexual person goes through with reassignment surgery.

In Emilee's case, her vagina never grew after the age of 4. All of the chemo and radiation treatments had stopped it from developing. Even though her social status had improved remarkably, she knew inside that dating was out of the question. What if someone found out?

> **"Whether your scars are visible or invisible,**
> **both are equally debilitating."**

Emilee made it through high school with an increased confidence. College came next. Emilee felt as though she was finally headed in the right direction.

"During my junior year of college, I was told that I was diagnosed with precancerous cells in my cervix. I had such plans for my future, which no longer included dying. But then I found out about the cells. It wasn't cancer, but I had been there before and didn't want to go back again."

The doctor suggested a hysterectomy and advised keeping one ovary for hormones so that she wouldn't launch right into menopause as a young woman. Even though Emilee had never had a period in her life due to the cancer treatments as a child, she was in favor of keeping as many of her body parts as possible.

"You will not be able to have children," the doctor told her.

When Emilee shared this with me, I cried for her.

———◆———

Author Note: When my second child was born, I knew something was wrong. At nine months old, he wasn't crawling; he just dragged his left leg behind him as he pulled himself along the floor. His body was floppy and he needed to be propped up with pillows to sit. I'll never forget the meeting with the Pediatric Neurologist.

"Your son will be at least half of his life behind. You should prepare for that."

There is something very connecting when you meet someone who has gone through a physical, mental, or emotional trauma. It's almost as though you are instantly part of the same tribe. All barriers fall away and you become fast friends regardless of beliefs, job title, economic status, or age in life. That's how it was with Emilee and me.

———◆———

As a society, we tend to think that some of the most successful people in the world are perfect. They must never have had challenges. After all, *The Telegraph* article talks about lack of career progression when you are affected as a child. But, this is not always the case. There is hope and, in many situations, the opposite can happen.

Here are just a few well-known people who have experienced challenges and have found ways to break through; to *shift* in order to thrive:

- Pete Peterson, the founder of Blackstone Group (who has since passed), raised a disabled son who now lives in a disabled facility in Northern California.
  - My son moved into the same facility four years ago.
- Stephen Hawking, one of the world's greatest Theoretical Physicists, has Lou Gehrig's disease, a motor neuron condition that eventually leads to full paralysis. He is in a wheelchair and speaks with the help of a computer.
- Richard Branson of Virgin Atlantic has dyslexia.

- Bram Cohen, the founder of BitTorrent, has Asperger's Syndrome.
- Actor Colin Farrell has a child with Angelman Syndrome, which can cause developmental delays, seizures and problems with movement and balance.
- Actor Greg Grunberg of the series *Heroes*, has a child with epilepsy.
- The Kennedy family had a child who was delayed and had a lobotomy.

The list goes on and on and on.

Does perseverance through trauma lead to super human success in life? According to the web source, greatergood.berkeley.edu, which explores the Science of a Meaningful Life, there is a theory that suffering can actually lead to success.

As quoted from the site:

In their new book, Supersurvivors, psychologist David Feldman and science journalist Lee Daniel Kravetz explain why some people seem to bounce back and even excel after trauma. Their book infuses the stories of "supersurvivors" with research findings that help uncover the individual traits or circumstances that help trauma survivors to experience "post-traumatic growth" rather than to suffer psychological setbacks.

According to Feldman and Kravetz, there are five factors that seem to help people transform suffering into positive change:

- *Hope*
- *Personal control*
- *Social support*
- *Forgiveness*
- *Spirituality*

So which is it? Failure or success when you grow up with a challenging condition or raise someone with one? Resolve or surrender? Who do you become? Which way do you shift?

Emilee had the hysterectomy.

She felt pretty worthless and thought that no man would ever want her. But, guess what, life is filled with shifts that lead us into all sorts of exciting directions.

Marriage was on her path after all, so life was looking up again. Then, she and her husband discussed children. Emilee knew that she couldn't have them, so they considered adopting, but a friend suggested they try a surrogate mom.

Emilee's hormones tested normal (she was thankful for one piece of her body chemistry remaining intact), so she and her husband agreed that they should try. They began the process of in vitro fertilization, which would involve an amazing surrogate mom (a Godsend according to Emilee) who would carry the child since Emilee did not have all of the internal parts to do so.

"The problem was, when they sucked the eggs out of my ovary, they were all black. I was losing hope."

It didn't make sense to the doctor though. How could hormone levels be normal, but the eggs not?

"The doctor paid for me to go to a specialist to see what was wrong."

The specialist had a hunch and performed an ultrasound on her stomach instead of her pelvis.

"That's when they found my other ovary, and that ovary was normal."

It just so happened that the doctor who performed the surgery to remove Emilee's cancerous tumor when she was four, saved an ovary and tucked it up above her stomach in order to get it away from the radiation. He was considering her future and the possibility that she might want to try to have children.

Hope returned.

The first time they went in with the needle, they were able to extract three eggs, all of which they fertilized and put into the surrogate mom. It didn't work the first time, but it did the second and their first boy was born.

Emilee and her husband were overjoyed and ended up going through the identical procedure a few years later with the same surrogate mother, and voila—twins!

Emilee entered a writing contest hosted by a pharmaceutical company and won $10,000 for her story about her miracle babies.

Life was great. The sadness and disease were behind her as she settled in with a blossoming family of five. Emilee continued to teach yoga and Pilates and worked on strengthening her own body, which had been through more than its share of invasion, pain, and suffering.

But, as we learn from our shifts, change can be just around the corner.

———◆———

"In 2014, I wasn't feeling well. My stomach was bloated, I was constipated, tired, and pretty achy every day. I knew something was wrong, but I ignored the signs. I just thought that I could never get cancer again."

Emilee began to bleed, which was particularly odd since she had never had a period in her life. Sex was painful and she was depressed.

"My body felt like menopause in full force; massive night sweats and all." She reluctantly decided to investigate.

Doctors performed a colonoscopy and a pap smear test, both of which came back normal. For all they could see, Emilee was fine. Friends and family told her to relax, that she was done with cancer. It was time to live life fully now.

Unfortunately, her marriage was unraveling at the same time and she would soon be on her own (not unlike her own mother). Yet, through it all, Emilee believed in following her intuition. With resolve, she began the search for what might be out of whack.

Another test showed what looked like a cyst on her ovary. The doctor didn't think it was ovarian cancer or anything like it. Just a cyst.

Ovarian cancer is known as the silent cancer because the signs are sometimes nonexistent. It only whispers. Even though there is a test for it, it is not completely reliable and is usually detected too late. But because of Emilee's persistence, they found that the cyst was actually a tumor (via a transvaginal ultrasound and rectal exam).

It was discovered one stage before too late.

"I remember the appointment with my doctor in January of 2015 when she told me that I had stage 3 ovarian cancer, and it was nasty. I was going to lose part of my colon *and* my lady parts."

Emilee wanted to die and she told the doctor so. She had been through this cancer thing too many times and simply didn't have any more energy left to fight.

"If the doctor hadn't grabbed me by the shoulders and said you have three beautiful miracle babies to live for, you can't die; I probably wouldn't be here today."

———◆———

No one wanted to do the surgery on Emilee because, basically, the belief was that everything in her pelvic region had to go. It would be a full exenteration. Tumors were everywhere: one on her sigmoid colon, one on her bladder, and one stuck between her rectum and posterior vagina.

On top of the tumors, there were a bunch of cancer cells all over her abdomen that had metastasized into the lining of her stomach and fatty pad (the omentum). Emilee's body was a mess and the topic of several leading oncologist's conversations.

Emilee was being prepared for the likelihood of a life threatening surgery. She was told that she probably would die; but, if she survived, life would never be the same. Pain would be her constant companion and she may not live that long anyway. She thought about the potential outcome for two months and couldn't get out of the fog.

The surgeon who finally agreed to go in told Emilee that she did not want to play God, so she asked for a second biopsy just to be sure.

"I didn't have to have the full exenteration. It would have taken everything, including my vagina. If I didn't die during the operation, I am sure I would have killed myself."

Thank goodness the second biopsy confirmed that I had ovarian cancer as opposed to cancer of the mullerion region, which meant that my entire pelvic area did not have to be removed.

Emilee got to keep most of her vital lady part. She didn't mind having her colon and everything else in the pelvis taken out during the 15-hour operation, just not the one part that would make her feel worthless if it was completely gone.

The collective decision was made to cut through the abdominal muscles (again) and remove the tumors as best they could. Emilee's exercise training focuses on the core. She had built her own stomach muscles back up after the many surgeries, but now they would have to be reopened. Emilee would have to start all over again.

The surgeon told Emilee that after removing much of her insides, she would have to create a full vagina by pulling the skin of Emilee's abs through her vagina. It was very complicated and highly likely that Emilee would not survive the operation and/or her vagina could close up.

Emilee fought for another chance at life.

———◆———

"After the chemotherapy and successful surgery, my mom showed up with a suitcase and stayed for nine months. She took complete care of me. I am still so appreciative of her help and will never forget her act of kindness."

During recovery, Emilee was limited in her ability to work. Without any salary and the responsibility of three children to raise, she lived by way of the generosity of strangers and friends via a GoFundMe account, all the while hoping that she would heal.

"I was beyond grateful for the financial aid from so many people who helped get me through the surgery and recovery, but inside I definitely felt detached and alone. I lost many friends because they probably didn't know what to say. Even my kids didn't want to be around me."

According to the National Cancer Institute, cancer-related post-traumatic stress (PTS) is similar to post-traumatic stress disorder (PTSD). Patients who learn that they have cancer have many of the same reactions as soldiers in the war zone:

- Repeated frightening thoughts
- Being distracted or overexcited
- Trouble sleeping
- Feeling detached from oneself or reality

"I knew that at some point I needed to work again in order to reconnect. So after a year, I did." At first, she just stopped by the studio in order to stay motivated. Then, she showed up to her Yoga and Pilates classes and personal client sessions with colostomy and catheter bags hanging off of her side.

Emilee could never tell if she was having a movement; so, if it happened during a private session, she would excuse herself to clean up. Sometimes it took 30-40 minutes. It became almost impossible to work. They had removed much of her intestines and you wouldn't recognize her vagina. But, Emilee showed up as best she could.

"You have to show up in life, regardless of the cards you are dealt."

During recovery, Emilee received an unsolicited email about becoming a certified life coach for *Living Your Life Story*™. It was an event that shifted her into who she is today.

"Suddenly I had hope again. Maybe I could beat this thing and help others who are recovering from cancer or have just found out that they have it. I can't die. I can't let my kids feel like their mom gave up. I won't cave in. I am going to fight and turn my life into serving others through Pilates, Yoga, and Life Coaching."

Emilee is full speed ahead. She has more Pilates clients than she can handle and a coaching business that is blossoming. She blogs and journals a lot and is thinking about writing a book. She has filmed hours of cancer core recovery exercises that are being turned into a video program online and via DVD.

Emilee has learned to forgive and move forward.

Her smile is as bright as ever.

"I don't know how long I will live, but I do know what I am meant to do with my career and life now. It took many shifts to get here, but I have found what makes me get up in the morning. My kids, my work, my life."

"I once thought of myself as a survivor, but now I see myself as a thriver...
My dream is to continue to inspire, encourage, and motivate through my
words, my coaching, and my teaching for many years to come"

Emilee has gone up against the odds—and won.

CHAPTER 2 TAKEAWAYS

- Live a life of love and joy regardless of what you have to face.
- Find a reason to live with purpose and you will learn how to live.
- Give back. Goodness will come back to you regardless of the path.
- When you face suffering, it's not the goal that matters. Get beyond where you are. That is enough.
- Life can seem like one giant struggle. It is part of the journey.
- Never give up, even if you desperately want to.
- Be courageous in life.
- Believe in yourself even if you have to fake it until you feel it.
- Make friends. Treasure them.
- When you finally find your purpose, share your journey.
- If you can channel unconditional love, you will be so happy that your actual job title won't even matter.
- Wonders never cease in life. You too are wonderful. Believe it.
- Shifting is a process; not a race to the finish line.

Chapter 3
SIMPLICITY

Amazon Achuar Tribe Warrior

Why would a remote indigenous tribe living in the middle of the Amazon rainforest make a shift in their life? They have drifted along, living simply and happily for generations.

Because the world around them is changing and, to put it bluntly, they have to.

Shifts are often needed during times of pain, survival, or exploration. For the Achuar, who analyze and believe in the visions of their dreams, they collectively dreamed of an exploration that continued to creep closer to them; so close that if they didn't make a shift, they could become extinct.

———◆———

I wanted to do something different—something so far outside of my comfort zone that it would help me shift into my own new life chapter. Or jolt me.

What could I do that was both exciting and scary at the same time?

I settled on the Amazon rainforest.

And so, along with eight other women I had never met, I signed up for the trip. I had no expectations other than to take it all in and just be myself. The whole idea of it was sort of romantic and freeing.

The week-long journey was organized by a non-profit organization called Pachamama, which has been leading philanthropic and purpose driven trips into the Amazon since the 70s. The goal is to bring people from the outside world in so they can understand the threats to the Amazon and tribes like the Achuar people, who live in the heart of the forest.

The Pachamama Alliance explains the journeys:

> By engaging you as a whole person—heart, mind, body, and soul—
> Pachamama journeys create an unforgettable experience that will inspire
> you for a lifetime.
>
> Journeys take place on the solid platform of relationships developed over
> many years by the Pachamama Alliance. We continue to be the primary
> partner to the indigenous groups in the region working toward the permanent
> protection of their lands and cultures. This trust allows for the most intimate
> access, as we are considered friends and allies, not tourists. You will learn
> firsthand about the challenges and visions of our indigenous partners, and
> how you can join them in ensuring this global treasure remains intact.

During our trip we were told that we would be visiting with, learning from, and participating in the ceremonies of the Achuar tribe. The Achuar tribe's

Shaman (spiritual leader) in the community we would be visiting was believed to have the power to analyze people's dreams and heal ailments of all sorts, including emotional. I was in.

———◆———

In preparation for the trip, I sprayed all of my clothes with a potent mosquito repellent, began ingesting a cycle of malaria pills a few days ahead and bought every kind of netting I could find so that I wouldn't get even one mosquito bite. I brought CIPRO along too, just in case I got really sick; but I was determined to stay healthy throughout.

During the informative group conference calls leading up to the trip, we were told to pack light and be prepared for very basic conditions. When I asked if I could bring a hairdryer, the woman hosting the call laughed.

"You won't be needing one of those in the Amazon. Don't bring it. But do bring sunscreen."

Confession: I did bring a hairdryer and I only used it once when we spent a few nights in an Eco Lodge. I blew out the generator that supplied electricity to the entire facility, but thankfully, they were able to restore it quickly. Sorry.

———◆———

We all flew into Quito, Ecuador from different cities and countries, joined up at a local hacienda, and met our Pachamama guide.

Cristina had a smile as wide as the equator. I liked her right away and was glad that she would be with us for the duration.

We took a seven-hour bus drive (I wore the ear patch that staves off car sickness, thank goodness. Others didn't fare so well) and arrived well after dark to a hacienda high in the Andes Mountains.

After a fantastic breakfast of local foods (plantains seemed to be a favorite) the next morning and an information discussion, we visited the actual center of the equator (which is in Quito) and then set off for another long ride to a quaint hotel that resided at the edge of the rainforest.

Another great meal followed with more information and discussion.

The following morning, we made our way to a small metal building that anyone would mistake for a storage shed. It was there that we crammed into three tiny prop planes for an hour-long flight to the center of the Amazon.

From the air, the rainforest looked like an endless array of broccoli florets—dense, various shades of green, untouched. It would take an awfully large pot to cook those beautiful looking veggies for dinner.

The problem is that companies are taking large swaths of the greenery away every day in their exploration for oil, and pharmaceutical companies are dissecting every plant and tree for base ingredients to add to potential cures for incurable diseases. The ecosystem is losing its balance and the people who live there are slowly being pushed out.

Many years ago, the Achuar dreamed of a threat to their habitat and began opening their way of life so that they might receive the help they need from the outside—so they can stay on the inside. I was on one of those educational experience campaigns.

———◆———

Every so often during our flight, we spotted an opening that hosted a strip of red dirt with palm thatched huts in clusters nearby. The open, homemade homes belonged to the tribal village communities and the strips of colored clay were the only way in and out.

"Here we go," the pilot said as we bumped and tossed our way down and toward one of the dusty patches. "Last week it rained, this was all mud and we couldn't land. You are lucky."

Lucky? I was pretty scared to be leaving all of civilization behind with no way out. The Amazon rainforest is only reachable by plane, followed by a river with many winding turns and, finally, on foot. Panic was on my mind.

———◆———

When we landed (thank goodness!), Diego, our local Achuar guide, was waiting for us. He was a young man, maybe in his 20s, wearing a simple shirt and a colorful, woven wrap that reminded me of a kilt minus the giant safety pin and fringes. I admired his blemish free, olive colored skin and thick, shoulder length black hair colored by the pitch night sky. I wondered how he kept it so shiny without shampoo or conditioner.

Diego donned tall rubber boots, which we were all given and told to wear during our entire time in the rainforest. If we stepped in mud, we would sink quickly, so the boots kept us clean and dry.

Diego lived in a community down the river. We learned that there were more than 60 of these communities with members ranging from 50 to 500 people. I liken them to little towns of huts and hierarchies that work similarly. Communities gather on a regular basis, with the local Shaman as the central figure.

"The forest is our hardware store, our grocery and our pharmacy."

Diego explained their use of and respect for the forest as we walked down a slippery bank to the murky, wide river and stepped into a motorized canoe. The long, carved transport hosted a green canvas cover to shield us from the heat, humidity, and powerful sun's rays. We were basically on the equator, so fair-skinned people like me had to take extra care.

Diego only spoke Achuar and Spanish. I don't speak either. The translation chain throughout our trip went something like this: The local village people we visited spoke Achuar to Diego, who translated in Spanish to Cristina, our Quito guide, who translated in English to our group. I enjoyed the attentiveness and respect each interpreter had for the person relaying the message. They never interrupted.

One of the remarkable things I noticed as we made our way to our lodging for the next four nights was the lack of noise; nothing but the sounds of nature and a small purr from the canoe motor that carried us along the curvy span of water.

We saw several brightly colored toucans that warrior chiefs kill to make their tribal warrior headbands. It takes a lot of toucan feathers to make just one. I didn't see an anaconda, which are known to be sleuthing in the waters, and thankfully no piranha either, although we were informed that they were there. I didn't put my hand in the water to confirm.

We did see the infamous pink dolphins, which exist in the fresh water of the Amazon. And yes, they are pink. We saw three of them playing not more than 100 yards from our canoe when we cruised around a bend in the river.

Pink dolphins were once thought to be bad luck, then good luck, and to have magical powers. No one in the Amazon hunts the pink dolphin; they respect them. I am glad they are safe, safer than the people that live above the banks of their home.

As for the bad luck, I never had any other than when I knocked out the power from my hairdryer. And the only mystical power I experienced during the entire voyage had to do with participation in the Ayahuasca ceremony (locally referred to as Natem).

(More on that later.)

We settled into a hand-built lodge that hosted smaller abodes of palm thatched roofs and raised planks above the unknown elements of the rainforest. Mosquito netting lined each hut and the beds within, but there were holes and I patched them by tying the netting together. The lodge was in need of a major upgrade, but it was better than sleeping outside, which we did do one night at the local Shaman's hut.

We met often in the grand room of the Eco Lodge to discuss the next day's agenda or eat our rainforest meals of plantain, fruit, simple meats, and local thick, pink juice drinks that were very sweet and slightly addicting.

The Achuar painted our faces with traditional warrior symbols and during other small windows of time we simply relaxed in the 90-degree heat.

There was a small bar tucked in the corner of the grand room where a few of us enjoyed a glass of wine and conversation at night. It must have been brought over by plane from Quito for visitors.

Internet coverage was practically non-existent, which helped the effort of unplugging from the outside world.

Our guide, Diego, stayed on the property. (He told us that he stayed for months at a time and then went back to his family in his community.) He was available at all meals and gatherings to answer questions and to tell us more about his tribal community (there are several tribes throughout the Amazon) and the threat that they all faced from outsiders. The dream and the hope was that

by opening their way of life, some of us might step forward to help keep the real intruders out—mainly the companies who want to flatten the land in order to drill for valuable oil beneath.

We went for a night hike and saw tiny little frogs (some poisonous), giant ants, and trees that actually moved. It was quite fascinating. Diego cut out a small piece (about the size of a quarter) from a particular tree with the machete that hung naturally by his side. He put the round piece on his hand and what looked like blood dripped across his palm and down his fingers. The Achuar use the bloody sap of the tree to heal wounds and scars. Maybe that's why his skin was so perfect.

He then placed the section back and patched up the tree, saying a few words of gratitude directly to the tree. Respect is a common theme in the Achuar culture.

———◆———

As I proceeded with the writing of this book, I kept coming back to the idea of respect.

When we make a shift in our lives, whether chosen or imposed, and when we incorporate the element of respect, we are bound to come out better on the other end.

For example, if we get hurt and we respect the doctors that heal us, we gain friendships, attention, better care. If we put it all on the line for our dreams and move forward with respect for all whom we encounter, our journey seems easier and more enjoyable. We gain new connections and a sense of belonging to something greater.

———◆———

Tradition goes hand-in-hand with respect for these great people, and we were lucky to experience several of their traditions firsthand.

One morning we met at 3:15 a.m. at the plank crossing that led to the river. I donned my mosquito spray and head net, which I cinched tight over my hat and, like my fellow travelers, secured a headlamp to light my way.

No one spoke as we made our way to the canoe and onto the quiet river. The forest seemed to be sleeping.

We travelled for close to an hour in complete darkness. Eventually, my eyes adjusted and I could see a small layer of fog or steam coming off of the river. Toward the end of the ride, I heard birds and scattering families of creatures along the banks and I saw monkeys in the trees.

The Amazon rainforest was peaceful and natural and beautiful and I couldn't understand why anyone would want to disturb it.

———◆———

We arrived at a bank along the river—I have no idea how they knew which one—and were greeted by women in long, handwoven skirts and t-shirts. Not a word was spoken.

I followed the group up to a flat dirt area where an enormous structure stood. The shelter reminded me of a giant, palm thatched hut on a Caribbean island beach resort, one with thick, hand-carved poles and no walls.

At the back of the large one room abode, I saw handmade wooden platforms with mosquito nets set around them. This was where the family slept.

In another corner was a compact, smoldering fire where a few women crouched on their bare feet around a large pot. Children huddled nearby, and chickens and tiny dogs roamed freely. It all seemed organized in a chaotic sort of way.

We were instructed to sit at the edge of the home on a long wooden bench. The plank looked like a split log that had been chipped away and worn to a smooth finish. Many people had sat there before.

The head of the family, a great Achuar warrior, was positioned across from us and next to another steaming pot. Diego was beside him. Cristina sat on the log with us—the women.

We were offered a special ceremonial tea that the Achuar women made and the men drank in a daily pre-sunrise ceremony. The women had consumed theirs before we arrived. To refuse the tea would be an insult.

I was given a carved out wooden boat that looked like a giant ladle with no handle and told to drink as much of the tea as I could. The more the better. The tribal leader was going to analyze our dreams, but we had to partake in the tea ceremony first.

What I didn't know was that after drinking the tea, we would be encouraged to throw up.

The Achuar throw up a lot. They do it every day. It is part of their ritual of purging in order to allow clarity. With clarity, they are able to interpret dreams accurately, see visions of what is to come, and heal.

Clarity is a strong word. When we are aware of, and notice all of the signs that line up to guide us toward a shift in our lives, we experience sudden clarity.

———◆———

When I wanted to work for one of the largest television networks in the country, I attended a party in New York City where the CEO of the network was standing in the middle of the ballroom with the President and a key member of the Federal Communications Commission. I was so nervous I wouldn't allow myself to acknowledge the shaking that had suddenly overtaken my body.

I marched up to the three of them, introduced myself, and told the CEO that I was going to work for him. Three months later, I did.

That was clarity. I knew what I wanted, where I wanted to go to move my career forward, and I went after it.

This is the kind of clarity the Achuar tribe has encapsulated. They want to keep their way of life intact but they know they need to make a shift in order to save it. Their dreams give them clarity as to the steps they need to make in order to do that. The tea ceremony is one of the traditions that brings such clarity.

———◆———

I took a deep breath and dipped my ladle in. The tea wasn't bad at all. It tasted like a mixture of weak, herb flavored water. Since it had been brewing for hours, we were told that it was safe to drink.

I drank three full ladles. Some women drank as many as eight.

Suddenly I didn't feel so well, so I got up and walked about 25 yards away from the hut and threw up behind a bush in the dirt. I could hear retching from all sides.

When I was sure that all of the tea was gone from my system and that I wasn't going to die, I returned to the bench and waited my turn.

The warrior leader asked each of us what we had dreamed the night before. Once the chain of translation reached him, he shared his interpretation with Diego in Achuar, who would make sounds like "mm, mm hmm, mm mm," throughout, in order to assure the chief that he understood the message.

Diego would then speak in Spanish to Cristina who would speak in English to each of us.

It amazed me how long the tribal leader and Diego would speak, but by the time the message got to us, the words were few. I need to learn more about the Achuar language.

When my turn came, I told the leader that I dreamt of flying through the sky.

After close to five minutes of translation, I was told that I was free and that I had hope for the future. My life was good.

I like the tea ceremony.

After the ceremony we were allowed to approach the women to see the beads and pottery they had made, as well as what was in the pot over the smoldering fire. More tea.

The women were all very shy. It was clear that men rule in this tribal community. But everyone is alright with it. There is order and it is clear. Everyone seems happy knowing their purpose and where they belong in the grander scheme of society. I found that refreshing. There was no posturing or infighting (at least from what I could tell). Life seemed peaceful, simple, balanced, and happy. Stuff was minimal. Conversation was essential and at the center. The community was connected.

Deep down we all want to connect in a meaningful way with our careers, our relationships, and with the communities in which we live.

According to an article in *Scientific American*, our need to connect with others is as important as food and water. We don't want to be or feel alone.

The Achuar are not alone. Families are large, animals roam freely, communities get together, the men laugh and chatter, the women huddle and whisper, the children listen intently and play simple games. It is lovely.

We watched the women harvest a white manioc root they use to make another drink that is only for the men. It is called Chicha. Chicha is a fermented beverage.

Women chew the manioc root and spit it into large containers; the saliva helps it to ferment. The men drink Chicha out of handmade bowls all day long, sometimes in place of meals or water. While I don't think it is as strong as alcohol, if it ferments too long, it does become more potent.

Chicha contains essential nutrients that the Achuar tribe's bodies need and you can find women hauling jugs of it everywhere they go. If a bug gets into a bowl of Chicha, the woman who made the batch removes the entire jug. They take pride in their Chicha.

Achuar men never venture to the gardens where Chicha is cultivated. Again, roles are defined and accepted readily.

As we shift in our careers, we take on roles and identities. Once we know what they are, like the Achuar, it is wise to accept them and embrace them; especially if they are aligned with our true purpose.

When we make shifts in our personal lives: whether we marry, we have children, we become empty nesters, our health changes, or someone passes; we must adjust and take on new roles. Embrace them and find ways to celebrate them and continue on the path toward a life of happiness. In a way our lives are always shifting, sometimes suddenly and other times gradually. If we accept and go with the flow of these shifts, we experience a happier existence.

It's like following the path of least resistance while acknowledging the signs that signal change.

We were lucky (maybe due to the respect we gave the tribal warrior/head of the home) to be offered the opportunity to watch him shoot a blow gun that was at least 6 feet long, and which contained poisonous tipped darts that are used to kill prey. He and his son were experts at hitting a coconut that was placed 30 feet away. I gave it a try. The weapon was very heavy. I missed the coconut and watched the dart impede itself in the dirt.

I don't think the women of the Achuar are warriors, so I am sure I wasn't judged for my lack of aim. At least I didn't hit anyone!

———◆———

**Amazon Achuar
Tribe Shaman**

Ceremony seemed to be emerging as the theme of our journey, so the next night we were invited to take part in the Ayahuasca ceremony at the home of the local Achuar leader.

We took another long canoe ride that afternoon and soon found ourselves at another bank of the Amazon where we were met by the community Shaman.

The experience began with a pre-ceremony ceremony.

The Shaman (also known as the medicine man or spiritual leader of the community) led us through the jungle in silence. He wore a colorful, hand woven ceremonial skirt, a loose fitting blue shirt, lots of beads and walked with bare feet, and a machete.

I walked behind him and watched as he chopped and slung away at vines that had taken over the jungle floor, only to reveal worn paths beneath. The bottoms of his feet were calloused and oblivious to the spikes and prongs that sprung up from the underbrush.

Along the way he often stopped at a tree, looked up, said a few words, and moved on. I felt his respect for the trees, yet couldn't help but wonder why this tree or that one? As I peered closer, I saw that the trees were taller and wider and had more roots than others. The branches stretched so far. Each one reminded me of the *Tree of Life* from the movie *Avatar*.

We walked for at least an hour in what felt like 100-degree heat and humidity. At times it seemed like we were going in circles.

We eventually arrived at a jungle bank that led down to a stream with a head high waterfall. I was about to faint from the heat, so was overjoyed when we were instructed by Cristina to take off our thick, hot, rubber boots, put on a modest bathing suit, and walk down to the river one at a time.

I hung my clothes and daypack on a tree branch, making sure not to let anything touch the ground. The ants were enormous.

When it was my turn, I put on flip flops, a pair of shorts and t-shirt, and carefully made my way down the slippery bank to the river's edge. Diego was waiting with a hand to help me into the water. I took off my sandals and stepped onto the river rocks below the rushing current. To my right was the waterfall and to my left was the Shaman, who sat on a rock ledge with his feet comfortably dangling in the water.

The process went like this: I walked up to the Shaman and snorted a combination of tobacco and water which he placed near my nose. Then, I turned around and stepped over to the waterfall. I dunked myself completely for the symbolism of purity (and to cool off!) and then I left. I was instructed to not look back at the Shaman. I climbed back up the sleek bank and changed back into my clothes. It was invigorating.

I was becoming a big fan of ceremonies. There is something comforting in ritual; whether it be religious practices, routines at home or work, or holiday traditions. Customs and practices give us a sense of belonging and of being part of something greater than ourselves.

When we make a shift in our career or personal lives, we develop new rituals and routines that guide us. If they feel right, we can be assured that we have chosen the right turn in the road.

I knew coming to the Amazon could be transformative for me personally, and I had a feeling that professional shifts were also in the works as a result of being invited into something local and intimate, yet global in purpose.

———◆———

We followed the Shaman back to the community and were given hours to wander, contemplate the beauty of the Amazon, and, when necessary, use nature as our bathroom. We were instructed not to eat anything after an earlier light meal of fruit.

The Shaman's hut was strategically situated high on a bluff overlooking the Amazon river so that he could see all of the canoes drifting by and any people approaching. He slept on a wooden platform with a rifle tucked next to him. I wondered how much he really slept each night.

He explained (through the chain of translation) that if a family was not happy with the Shaman's healing efforts, it was not uncommon for the family to try to kill the Shaman. So while being a Shaman is a revered role that takes years to obtain—from receiving the calling to living in the Amazon forest alone for years—there is risk.

The Shaman is the main interpreter of dreams and the one who knows all of the plants and roots of the forest that heal physical ailments, emotional conditions, and help to interpret dreams. Everyone comes to the Shaman like a person would go to a doctor, psychiatrist, or pharmacist.

———◆———

As night fell, the festivities began.

The entire community seemed to be present to watch the Americans partake in the sacred Ayahuasca ceremony. Women and children were huddled on platforms and men sat in distant circles drinking Chicha and talking energetically. I think it was about their current dilemma as a people.

A row of small mats covered with mosquito netting had been set in a row on the dirt. This was where we would sleep at the end of our experience.

A small circle of carved wooden stools, ending with a crude table representing the head of the circle was where the ceremony took place. We took our seats in anticipation of what was to follow.

The Shaman had disappeared for much of the contemplation time, but when it was too dark to see, he appeared and sat at the table, placing what looked like a giant plastic Pepsi bottle on the platform.

The liquid inside looked like mud.

According to an *Introduction to Ayahuasca*, Ayahuasca is an Amazon plant mixture that induces altered states of consciousness, which can last between four to eight hours after drinking it. It is used as a medicine and as a shamanic method of communication, usually in a ceremonial capacity. The core ingredient is a vine called banisteriopsis caapi, which means vine of the soul. A second ingredient can be either chacruna or chagropanga, which are plants that have a high level of N-Dimethyltryptamine or DMT, a psychedelic substance. The Ayahuasca mixture can be mild or potent.

I didn't know what to expect. Would I hallucinate? Would I see familiar things? Would my purpose in life be revealed to me? I was excited for answers, but in a way, didn't expect any either.

I ended up seated next to the table and when the Shaman appeared, he said some things to the group, poured about four ounces of the thick liquid into a small wooden cup and started to whisper and whistle to it. This lasted for about a minute and then he handed it to me.

Oh great. I was first.

I drank the murky substance (it tasted pretty bad), said thank you, and gave the small dish back to him. I waited in silence. Nothing happened.

The woman to my left went next. She was twice my size so I figured that it would hit me faster. I was wrong. By the time the third person was done drinking their portion, number two asked to lie down. Cristina (who we all called Cuqui) and another helper (I think Diego) guided her to a long banana leaf in the dirt. We each had one waiting for us and that is where we would experience the effects of the potion until it was time to go to sleep.

----●----

Suddenly and without warning, I didn't feel so well.

"Cuqui, I need to lay down too," I called out to the dark night sky, which hosted stars in the zillions. I swear I saw at least 100 shooting stars every minute.

I was led to the leaf near my new friend and was glad for the reclined position. I kept my eyes open because I didn't want to miss a thing. I watched as brilliant dots flew across the sky, only to burn out after their trek. So many stars…

After about…well, I don't really know how long, I saw something amazing. It was a face of a clown with a hat on. But the clown looked tribal. It was brightly colored too. Reds, blues, yellows. I watched with amazement as it made a full circle in the sky, a perfect circle, and then disappeared. It looked something like this, but with brilliant colors:

Very cool, I thought to myself. I am awake and aware and am seeing something totally fascinating in the sky. My limbs felt heavy, almost paralyzing. I was later told that Ayahuasca can make your body lumbered and uncooperative. Basically, it is a form of poison that can cause serious nerve damage if you don't throw it up once it takes effect.

Not again.

Cuqui and several helpers came over to me at what felt like every few minutes and asked me if I had to throw up.

"No, I'm good," I replied.

I looked into the sky and now saw what looked like a pinball game of a bunch of geometric squares all lined up together across the sky. Each one was brilliantly colored and lit up and they were all moving, with little colored balls and bouncing dots.

Next, I saw what looked like a giant cross of blue and red dots. It filled the entire expanse above me. When I leaned over to look at my friend on the banana leaf next to me, I was convinced that she was texting her kids on her cell phone, but the pattern on her screen was the cross of dots that I saw in the sky. I think I called out that there was no internet reception in the Amazon, but she didn't pay attention.

Then, I didn't feel so well.

"I have to throw up," I said to no one and suddenly four people were hovering over me.

"I like privacy if that's okay."

"Sure," they all replied and backed away, but when I got up on an elbow, I could see that they were watching me out of the corner of their eyes.

I wonder if Ayahuasca makes you paranoid or if that is a personal trait I needed to heal. I never thought of myself as paranoid; Well, I had left my marriage and wondered at times if my husband was having me followed. I think I had trust issues that needed addressing.

According to an explanation of the healing traditions associated with the people of the Amazon, there is emphasis on an effort to balance the masculine and feminine within us. They believe that both physical and psychological unbalances are related to past compromises we have made with one of these archetypes.

I started to ponder the roles I played in all of my careers and in my personal life.

In business, I could be tough and stand up to any man, but I remained a woman. I never felt the need to be a man in a man's world. I felt balanced there.

In my personal life, however, I felt that I was pushed toward the masculine, which means confidence without arrogance. I really wanted to align more with the feminine side of my life where I trusted my heart and intuition. I knew that my creativity and purpose lied there and I had felt stifled. I was on a journey to discovering who I really was underneath and felt it was time for that part of me to take center stage. I love my children and wanted to continue to nurture them and my relationship with each of them. I also wanted to nurture myself. I was gaining clarity.

I next saw a Pinocchio-type of face with a bald head and glasses. I watched as the nose grew in length. I obviously didn't have faith or belief in someone. The face was familiar. Then, it turned scary and I looked away.

I later researched faces that one might see while experiencing the Ayahuasca. They almost always get ugly as though we need to face our fears and tell them to go away. Once we do that, we feel at peace, tranquil, transformed. We gain clarity and courage and are more in line with our authentic self.

I told the ugly face that I didn't want to see it anymore and it disappeared.

Sometimes in our work, we are confronted with the faces of people (many times our own boss) who are mean or are micro managers. We need to let them rant on, not react, and align ourselves with our true nature. When we do this, even the most contentious of work environments becomes tolerable. Eventually, we find our shift and our way out of those situations, or we stand up to the bully and come to an understanding. Sometimes, we even develop empathy for their pressure and plight. Other times, we change due to empathy and understanding.

It was time to purge my system of the poison. I leaned up on one elbow and tucked my shirt away from the dirt so that I didn't end up tossing my insides onto it. I helped myself throw up by sticking my finger down my throat. You could say I was slightly concerned about making sure I got all of the concoction out of my system.

It was then that I saw the soft little creature that had settled in next to my leaf. It was a cross between a guinea pig and a marmot. It had giant white eyes and soft fur and was about seven or eight inches long. I began to pet it.

"Hi Buddy," I said as he wiggled with pleasure at my touch. "I know you are not real, but you sure are cute."

A helper came over to me.

"Are you okay? Who are you talking to?"

"Oh, this little creature is hanging out with me. It's okay, I know it's not real, but it sure looks real." The helper smiled and moved on to the next leaf.

"I know you're just a hallucination, but maybe you should go back to your mama, your family." The creature stayed put.

Each time I threw up (which was many), I saw the little creature that never left my side.

I continued to see visions of colors and faces and bright pleasant geometric patterns. I didn't see snakes or anything evil, other than the faces that turned mean before they disappeared or I told them to go.

I closed my eyes briefly and heard a bunch of dried leaves being shaken over my body. The shaking leaves, which sounded like a garbage bag being snapped open, were accompanied by soft chants and intermittent whistles.

The Shaman was healing me.

"Cuqui, tell the garbage bag to stop," one of the women yelled. I chuckled. She didn't know and the Shaman passed her by. She wasn't ready for healing I guess.

Eventually, the visions subsided and when I turned to throw up once more, my little friend was gone.

A helper came over to me and told me it was time to go to bed. How did they know?

I was guided to my mat where I wrapped the mosquito net tightly around me and fell asleep.

It's hard to explain the calm and clarity that I
experienced at that moment. I felt like I knew myself
better than I ever had before and I was happy.
I had shifted.

The next morning, we were given a light breakfast of fruit and were told to sit in a circle in the Shaman's hut. For the next hour or so, we were asked to tell him about one of our visions, which he would interpret.

Some of the women had no visions at all and even went back for seconds or thirds of the Ayahuasca in an attempt to encourage an experience.

In at least one case, the Shaman said they were trying too hard.

Good lesson to learn about life in general.

When we try too hard at anything, whether it is performing in our work, creating a work of art, or trying to move a relationship forward, we are often blocked or met with temporary failure. Yet, when we just let go and go with the flow, ideas and progress always seem to come.

It was my turn.

I told him about the creature near my leaf and he smiled.

"This creature came from mother earth. You are being watched over at all times. Everything is going to be okay."

Just the words I needed to hear.

My life was going through a transition and I was anxious about the eventual settlement of my divorce, as well as my future financial and career direction. Just hearing the Shaman's words gave me comfort.

Everything has been more than alright ever since and I have great clarity for even greater things that lie ahead.

As for the Achuar tribe (and others like them throughout the Amazon Rainforest), they continue to have visions and seek clarity as to what they should do to preserve their way of life, their land, and their existence.

Oil drilling was voted in by the Ecuadorian government in 2013 and, now, one third of the rainforest is being auctioned off for oil drilling in order to alleviate the debt of Ecuador. The indigenous tribes are not in agreement. Peru has complained that oil drilling has polluted and caused imbalance in the rainforest's ecosystem.

The visions and dreams continue and advocates are out in force to help the people of the rainforest figure out what their shift must be in order to maintain their course of life. Will they have to change with the natural course of advancement in the world or will they be able to halt progress so that they can continue their traditions and way of life?

Shifts aren't always easy and may not seem to have happy endings; yet, we learn so much when we do shift and when we adapt to that shift, we can find happiness. The Achuar may have to be happy in a smaller space, or they may have to come out in force to fight for their beliefs and claims.

You can be sure that the many Shamans throughout the forest are heavily involved in interpreting the course of action.

Chapter 3 Takeaways

- Pay attention to your dreams; they will help you make sense of your current situation and learn how to move forward.
- Respect our planet. It is all we have.
- Be part of a community. Find your tribe. You will find love and purpose.
- Follow your heart, regardless of what opposition you face.
- Live simply and thrive.

PART TWO

WHEN TO SHIFT

"To improve is to change; to be perfect is to change often."
—Winston Churchill

Improve

: *to increase in value, excellence*
: *to become better*

We make choices every day. Choices with consequences. Choices that lead to success or failure.

When the consequences are the difference between life and death, we decide to make a shift in order to survive, or not.

Suffering can lead to shifting.

When the choices are less subtle, like crossing the street or eating a kale salad instead of a fast-food burger for lunch, we are seemingly on automatic. But, if we choose to cross the street against the red light and not in a crosswalk, that is a much riskier choice and a shift may happen to us. If we eat the wrong food for too long, it may be time to make a shift in our actions, our behavior, and, eventually, our life.

When it comes to your career, you might think that everyone shifts due to money. That is not necessarily the case. Pensions are disappearing, the gold watch upon retirement is rare and job security is not a given. You may need to make a shift because you don't have the proper work/life balance. You may never see your kids, can't take a vacation, work 110 hours a week. That is out of sync.

Usually there is an incident that propels the timing of a shift: a new baby, a health condition, no clear direction at your current job.

If you listen to your inner voice, you will know. If you follow the path that seems to make the most sense and makes you feel that it is right, you should shift toward it.

If your attitude or sense of self is negative, degrading, and depressing, and you simply can't get out of it, then you definitely need to shift to a happier place. It is best to meditate and not act on anything until you feel strongly that a change needs to occur.

If you are drifting along and something happens *to you* that is out of your control, you will blatantly know that it is time to make a shift. Your approach will need to change and when you begin to change, you need to have continuous faith that you will come out better on the other side.

I believe that we all need to make shifts in our lives at some point along the way in order to find balance, meaning, and happiness.

In the next few stories, we learn when it made sense for these amazing people and what moved them toward taking concrete action.

When something matters to you so much, or bothers you so much, or motivates you so much you can barely contain it, you should consider making a shift.

Chapter 4
FINDING NORMAL

Andy Wirth – CEO-Squaw Valley and Alpine Meadows Resorts

A ndy was alone in the vineyard.

Endless rows of vines, each stripped of their ruby red clusters, surrounded him. The knotty branches stretched out quietly now, held still by thick strands of wire as they patiently waited for the field hands to tend them.

"I looked down at the glob of flesh gathered at my wrist and a detached arm and knew my chances were slim, but I couldn't really move. All I could do was watch as the ground turned into a pool of a dark cabernet."

Like the vines, he hoped that someone would come to tend to him—soon.

www.outsideonline.com

Andy loved to jump.

He welcomed the pressure of mother nature against his skin while freefalling from 14,000 to 2,000 feet before throwing the chord that would deploy his parachute and jolt him upward. The pillowed glide was a bonus to an exhilarated rush of flight, and when his feet connected with the earth, he couldn't wait to do it all over again.

But this day was different.

Andy and his buddies, JT Holmes and Timy Dutton (nicknamed Rubber Ducky), were excellent skydivers, which meant that they would jump last out of the plane so that they could fall longer and glide further to the landing zone. Sometimes that meant inverted exits from the plane (flying upside down) and other complex formations. Excellence requires skill and the three friends had it in spades.

Timy was a professional skier and base jumper, and JT a professional skier, base jumper, and skydiver. JT had been in several movies as a stunt man and had been interviewed by Anderson Cooper on *60 Minutes* to discuss his newest endeavor on the legendary Eiger in Europe, where he would ski a section of the Eiger in a contiguous series of moves which have never been done before, then speed fly (skiing with a canopy) in another section, and then finish with a ski base jump and fly a canopy to the valley floor.

Base jumping was something Andy couldn't wait to try.

Flying with friends like the legendary skydiver Charles Bryan, Chris Boyle, and his friends Timy and JT meant maneuvers that would add complexity and variety, something that they all gladly explored. Sometimes, they would press hands to their sides and shoot through the sky like arrows in order to dive faster, a maneuver called delta tracking. Other times, they soared, freefalling together at 120 miles per hour, clasping hands in midair, and laughing at the high of it all.

"We liked to fly in formations after doing four-way inverted exits."

The friends were comfortable *and* fearless.

———◆———

Equal to the thrill of flight, love and respect for nature has always been part of Andy's DNA. His grandfather, Conrad Wirth, ran the National Park Service for Presidents Eisenhower, Kennedy, and Johnson.

Andy had always dreamed of following in his grandpa's footsteps and, when he was a young boy, he listened intently to his ancestor's words; words he would need that day.

No matter what adversity you face, act.

———◆———

Andy followed his grandfather's advice in everything he did. As a trained EMT and Back Country High Angle Rescue Ranger, Andy developed the tools to aid the injured that were stuck in hard to reach situations—the tools he needed when it came time to act.

He was often first on the scene in climbing accidents, for example, where he came across contorted bodies in hard to reach places. Andy often had to treat them and keep them from going into shock—all without medication.

"Words can be very powerful when it comes to saving lives."

He would tell the injured to look at him and he would talk to them in calm, commanding tones. Andy told them how to breathe in order to slow down the panic that could bring on the tragic, life ending condition of shock; all while doing his best to stabilize them until medical help arrived (if it could)—all with words.

Andy later shifted from back country rescue to the ski industry, which kept him connected to nature. He climbed the ladder to CEO of Steamboat, a destiny Colorado Ski Resort and, more recently, the President and CEO of Squaw Valley Ski Holdings (Alpine Meadows | Squaw Valley) in Lake Tahoe, California.

Along the way, Andy developed into an accomplished athlete who trained for triathlons in the hills and waters of the Colorado and Sierra mountains. He expertly skied the peaks of both ranges and absorbed the space between the earth and clouds each time he jumped out of a plane. His fitness was on par with someone half his age.

———◆———

The winds were kicking up that morning so the group had to move from Davis to Lodi in order to avoid potential wind outbursts. Confidence was high.

"From the ground, it looked like a gust came up," Andy's good friend Rich, who had come along, recalled. "It didn't look good. They were either going to hit electrical lines or a vineyard. Everyone guided their chutes 90 degrees to avoid the wires in the sky or the ones on the ground. Everyone except Andy."

———◆———

Every decision we make in life is a choice. Sometimes we make good ones. Other times we don't. Either way, we must accept the consequences of our actions, which shift us in a new direction or along a path toward a goal or purpose. The key is to act, no matter the outcome. If we don't act, we simply don't move forward toward who we are meant to be.

Of the three friends, Andy pulled his chute first, which allowed him to float longer. When it came time to decide if he should change direction in order to avoid being electrocuted or potentially torn up, he figured that he had more time than the others and could make it over the vineyard.

He didn't.

A large stake holding up the wires that tied the vines caught Andy's arm. In an instant, the steel ripped through his flesh and pushed it, along with muscles and tendons, down his arm to the edge of his wrist. Essentially, his right arm was detached.

Mother nature left a little patch along the tricep and covering his hand; but everything else was bone. Blood gushed from his brachial artery and Andy was fading fast.

He looked down and said to the air, "I am in a rough spot."

"It was happenstance that the song *Just Breathe* by (Pearl Jam's) Eddie Vedder drifted in and out of my consciousness. It was something I would say to others I was stabilizing while a backcountry ranger and the song seemed to be a way for me to apply the same advice to myself. I started to sing it out loud.

Yes, I understand
That every life must end.
As we sit alone,
I know someday we must go.

"Ironically, the lyrics seemed to fit my condition."

Stay with me.
Let's just breathe.

"In a way the song helped me to not be afraid of death; after all, we all die. Yet, I still had the will to live and knew that, if I could just breathe, I wouldn't go into shock. Shock kills people. I knew keeping shock at bay was the key to making it."

Trauma was not foreign to Andy. He knew what to do—he just couldn't do it.

In addition to a shredded arm, the chords on Andy's parachute were entwined on the metal stake, which inhibited his range of motion. But he did have logic and his grandpa's words, which would have to do.

"My EMT training wanted to take control of the situation, organize my thoughts, come up with a plan, and then act if I didn't want to die—and I didn't want to die. On the other hand, I knew the likelihood of dying was exceedingly high since I couldn't figure out a way to stop the bleeding. Do I accept it or fight it? I either die in pain, but at peace, or fight to live and know that the road to recovery, regardless if my arm could be saved, would be very long. From my experience, I knew that if I could make it to a flight nurse in a flight-for-life helicopter, I would have the chance. I have seen flight nurses do incredible things in really bloody, gnarly situations. That became my goal…make it to the helicopter."

Andy was well aware that if he lost too much blood he would die. He had to stop, or at least slow, the bleeding.

Because he was tangled, as well as injured, Andy couldn't reach over his body to make a tourniquet like he was taught to do. He had to come up with Plan B.

When someone is in a dire situation, it has been reported over and again that they find super human strength to do what must be done in order to survive or save a loved one.

Andy came up with an idea that would be so painful it could kill him. But it was his only hope and the only strategy he could think of to (hopefully) prevent his demise long enough for help to come.

Balling his left hand into a tight fist, Andy rocked his mangled body back and forth until he gained enough momentum to roll over and swing his left arm. With one giant thrust, he jabbed his fist into the armpit below his right shoulder where the axillary artery resides.

The sheer pain almost made him pass out, but he didn't. Instead, from somewhere near the center of his core, Andy let out a wail akin to a parent seeing their dead child. The sound bounced off the silent, beauty surrounding him and scared him so much that he gained focus—and began to yell.

"I am here! Someone come! Please!" He mouthed the words of "Just Breathe," and then sang it as loud as he could.

"What did you think of during that time, aside from the pain and the song that helped you hang on?"

"Dying. Never seeing my kids, my wife, or my friends again. I still had so much that I wanted to do on this earth. I knew right then that if I made it, I would never take time for granted. I would act in all things and make my life the best it could possibly be. I also knew that I would likely be part of a new group—the disabled—whether I had one or two arms, and I would do all I could for them."

SHIFT.

One of the other skydivers on the plane had seen Andy land and had been trying to find him for a good half hour.

"I'm not sure how long I was there in that vineyard, but it seemed like forever. And then I heard my name."

When the fellow diver found him several rows deep in a vineyard ditch, Andy breathed a little more easily. He just might have a chance. He told her how to make a tourniquet out of his altimeter, which she did as best as she could.

Andy's wife and friends arrived next.

"After the dive, we saw three guys walking toward the landing zone. At first we thought they were our friends and all was well," Andy's friend Rich explained. "But as they got closer we realized that they were actually some of the other divers—and we knew something was up. I think I was going about 100 mph to get to the vineyard area where we now thought Andy had landed."

Rich pushed through rows of vines calling Andy's name.

"Rich is that you? Is my wife with you? Tell her to stay back."

Rich understood why.

"Blood was spurting everywhere. It reminded me of a slaughtered cow. I didn't realize that a human could have that much blood in him."

Andy did his best to remain calm through the pain as the other diver finished the tourniquet and ran for help. Rich tried to talk to Andy in the same calm manner while telling Andy's wife to stay back, all the while wondering if Andy would make it.

The ambulance arrived soon after. They had to park on the access road and enter in a back way to reach him. Rich watched as the two paramedics cut the flight suit away and expose the de-gloved arm. Andy's elbow was pointing in an unnatural direction and his arm had to be set.

"S***," one of the paramedics said. He didn't have an extra set of gloves, which meant that the other paramedic could not touch the damage.

"I'll do it," Rich replied. Rich followed the instructions of Andy and the paramedics so that Andy's arm could be set properly for transport.

"I basically had blood all over me. Then, they had to move him onto the gurney," Rich winced.

"Okay, guys, I need some oxygen. You are losing me," Andy told the paramedics. He knew he was close to death.

As they were about to transport him, Andy told them to lift him up on his feet first. Not a great idea. "That really hurts. Let's not do that again," Andy instructed.

"He was like a coach to the team working on him." Rich marveled, and was amazed at how calm Andy was being. "Andy basically saved his own life that day."

Timy showed up next. No one knew where JT was, so Timy went to find him in case he too was injured.

JT was a mile down the road and was fine. The entire plane load of skydivers was caught off guard by the changing winds and all were scattered.

By the time JT arrived, it was time to go. The two paramedics, Rich and JT carried the gurney and shimmied their way through the narrow vineyard ditches until they got to the ambulance. It was like carrying dead weight.

A sheet was placed over Andy's arm so that no one could see it, including his wife, who Andy did not want to upset any more than she understandably already was.

"Just before we loaded Andy into the ambulance, he looked me straight in the eye," Rich recalled. "Don't let them take my arm," he said. "Do all you can to save my arm."

When the ambulance made it down the road and around the corner, the airlift helicopter was already waiting.

"Was there a point where you stopped thinking about death?" I asked Andy.

"What made me finally realize that I was going to make it was the sound of the helicopter. The flight for life rescue crews are the best in the business. I was going to live."

Rich completed the story.

"As he was being loaded onto the helicopter, I told the crew that Andy was strong, an athlete, and that he will make it. They needed to do all they could to save his arm."

Rich will never forget the look on the face of one of the crew members.

Not good.

As the helicopter readied for flight, Rich heard Andy talking to the flight nurses. "Save my arm, do all you can, please save my arm."

"The single most powerful moment of that afternoon came at the moment they loaded me," Andy told me. "I heard the turbines of the helicopter spin up. They slammed the door shut. I looked over to the flight nurse with his helmet and visor down and said 'I have given everything I have to get here…it's all on you now…I am out of the fight now.' At that moment, I looked back to the door and the sun shone so brightly in my eyes. I had a chance to live to the next day. Now I can rest. The song *Just Breathe* stopped."

———◆———

Many stories have been told about facing death and coming out on the other side as someone new. It is like a rebirth, an extreme shift that makes us consider and take action toward who we really want to be in the world.

In his book, *Life after Life*, Raymond Moody actually interviewed over 100 people who had near-death experiences resulting from major traumas. He discovered that after such a close call, many became more loving toward others and much less focused on their own material success.

———————◆———————

Andy has a longtime friend from Wyoming named Buck Brannaman. Buck is considered to be the original horse whisperer and was the inspiration for Nicholas Evan's book and movie, *The Horse Whisperer*, directed by and starring Robert Redford. Redford brought Buck on the set to consult during the filming of the movie.

A documentary was also made about Buck, called *Buck*. It tells of his painful life and how he channeled his pain into compassion, which led to his ability to be the horse whisperer.

According to Andy, Buck is a *real* horseman; raising and starting horses, branding cattle, and keeping the traditions of the true cowboy alive. But, Buck went through a lot along the way, including being physically and mentally abused by his father, getting sent to foster care, and running away.

"He often slept in the kennel with the dog when he was young," Andy continued. "Yet, Buck has become such a remarkable man, dialed in and solid, and has always been a source of inspiration to me on what it means to experience a living death and to come out the other side a better man."

Andy described how all of the abuse Buck experienced made him yearn for compassion, which he never got, but fully gave to the horses. The horses gave back by letting Buck understand their feelings and train them with ease.

Buck developed paramount empathy through personal pain.

"Your horse is a mirror to your soul.
Sometimes you might not like what you see...
Sometimes you will."
—Buck Brannaman

Buck continues to work with horses and is a highly sought after speaker about sensitivity and compassion.

"If Buck could make it through all of his pain, I could make it through months in the hospital and 25 reconstructive surgeries." Andy's physical life was surely about to shift, but what he didn't realize at the time was that his emotional approach to life would shift exponentially, too.

Andy's path to recovery has included 26 reconstructive operations. There may be more.

"I have scars, skin grafts taken from most parts of my body and I have no lats. I don't have much feeling in the middle part of my arm, but I am here and I am grateful."

It was a long time before Andy could do anything. He went through physical therapy twice a day and continues to rehab even though he was back at work after only 51 days.

Andy says that his skydiving days are likely over.

On April 29, 2014, Timy Dutton died in a sky diving accident at the same location where Andy almost lost his life. Andy was not with Timy that day. According to reports, Dutton and another skydiver from Lake Tahoe collided in mid-air during the dive. Dutton was knocked unconscious before he was able to pull his chute. Andy was heartbroken and remains so to this date.

In addition to Timy Dutton, Andy has had several friends die while doing extreme sports, which has given him pause.

His friend Erik Roner died in a skydiving accident during a Squaw Valley fundraising event. Erik hit a tree on the way down and was dangling unconscious from him parachute. When rescuers reached him, he had already passed. Erik was a regular on MTV and Outside Television. Andy recalled how Erik had been buried in an avalanche only a few months prior and almost didn't make it then.

Another friend was Johnny Flores, a world record-holding base jumper who died during parachute exercises in preparation for an extreme sports tournament. He died on Mount Titlis in Engelberg, Switzerland.

———◆———

"How has your mental and emotional state changed since the accident? I know the physical challenges have been very real," I asked gently.

"Life is simpler now and I appreciate it so much. I just got back from spending time in Colorado with my daughter who I hadn't seen in a year. It was the best visit ever and we are now in constant communication. As I think about life on a daily basis, in addition to family and friends, there are three things that make me happy: exercise, the outdoors, and the environment."

Not long ago, Andy went on an overnight backpacking trip into the Sierras with friends. He carried 80 pounds on his back. Even though he needed help getting the pack on, he was determined to be the best warrior he could.

He also did a road bike ride from Steamboat Springs, Colorado, to Park City, Utah. Four hundred miles in four days. He had to stop several times to adjust the brace on his arm and take some pain medication, but he did it.

I don't think Andy will ever give up his love of exercising in the outdoors, despite his condition. His athletic pursuits, like IRONMAN triathlon, are his way of trying to find his way back to normal, as he says.

———◆———

In addition to working to protect the environment in the Sierras, joining Squaw and Alpine Ski Resorts in an effort to provide a beautiful and seamless outdoor experience for skiing enthusiasts, and focusing on his recovery, Andy is committed to helping anyone who has experienced injury, trauma, or disability. He understands them, empathizes with them, and includes them.

"We all matter in life. We are all important.
The least of us all is the person that matters the most. We should all care."

Andy has gained particular respect for groups such as the wounded veterans, as his ability to understand and identify with them is enhanced by his accident. Andy helped form a team, called *Special Warfare Warrior*, which honors and supports wounded veterans by helping them enjoy the mountains and build up their self-esteem and confidence. The suicide rate of men who return from war is high (more than 22 die a day) and Andy wants that number to fall to zero.

"We generate support for the Navy SEAL Foundation, a group that provides immediate and ongoing assistance to the Naval Special Warfare Community and its families. We have 20 warriors coming this weekend from the military to the mountains. We want them to enjoy nature, challenge their limits, and know that they matter. They are going to have a blast."

At Squaw and Alpine mountains, Andy lowered the price of a season ski pass for active military to $25, with all of the proceeds going to support the program which brings these warriors to the mountain. They deserve to enjoy the mountains, be supported as they seek to adjust to a greatly transformed life and be honored for their service.

The ski challenge programs have been expanded from Alpine to include Squaw, in order to help people of all injuries (physical or other) learn to ski and enjoy what the mountains have to offer them in terms of healing.

"As I've worked through my recovery, I've often thought of the challenges through which these incredible men and women and their families have navigated. Their stories and courage have certainly motivated and encouraged me. From them, I've learned that courage is not when one has the *strength* to press on; courage is found when, in the *absence of strength*, one finds a way to advance…to press on."

I saw the tears in Andy's eyes when he talked about his love for his kids, the vets, the disabled, the recovered (and still recovering), the earth and life itself. Even with all of his challenges, Andy is a warrior.

⎯⎯⎯◈⎯⎯⎯

And as for the Eddie Vedder song that helped Andy through the biggest shift in his life?

"Eddie heard about my story and how I relied on the words of *Just Breathe* to sustain me, to keep me alive. He invited me to one of his concerts and I got to meet him backstage. I am convinced that Vedder's song kept me alive that day."

Andy picked up his guitar again. He is relearning Eddie's song, albeit with a very modified arm.

Chapter 4 Takeaways

- When in doubt, act, always act.
- Adventure outside your comfort zone, regardless of the end result.
- Just breathe.
- Give back.
- Let empathy be your guide and approach life with an open heart.
- Appreciate life. Embrace it. You matter in this world.
- We all face roadblocks in life; the goal is to find your own normal and be happy there.
- The road to success has many parking spaces—keep driving.
- Do something with your intellect. Influence, advocate, and affect change.
- Have a purpose in life that is more than money or station.
- Stay connected.
- Pay attention to preparation and what comes across your path. Your experiences will serve you when you least expect it.
- Whenever you can, choose to act in the interest of our society and our environment.
- Survive. Act. Live.

Chapter 5

ALLEVIATE SUFFERING

**Jerry Colonna – CEO, Venture Capitalist, Life Coach,
Start-Up Boot Camp Leader, Peaceful Warrior**

J erry held the kind of high profile positions that most people only dream
of reaching.

After a successful career in publishing and as a leading Venture Capitalist,
he became a senior member of JPMorgan Partners (JPMP), the private equity
arm of JPMorgan Chase.

When it came to betting on up and coming companies, Jerry decided who and what to invest in. He loved it.

The problem was, he didn't love himself.

"I was depressed at 38 and wanted to kill myself. It was the second time in my life I wanted to do that. The first was an attempt at 18... I'm not telling you anything I wouldn't say in public."

Growing up wasn't easy for Jerry. He lived in a violent household as the sixth of seven kids. His mother was in and out of mental institutions due to possible bouts of schizophrenia and his father was an alcoholic. Money was scarce.

Jerry had to figure out how to rise above the pain. Or escape it.

"I told myself that I couldn't be alone in my suffering; there had to be other people like me, but where were they?"

At a young age, Jerry was on the hunt for self-love—a way out of depression, the guilt from being abused, and the shame of not being able to fix his family.

According to studies reported by the American Counseling Association, when a child suffers trauma, the lasting effects of the trauma can last well into adulthood. Depression, anxiety, guilt, shame, and suicidal thoughts are byproducts. Whether abuse is sexual, verbal, or physical, it really doesn't change the collateral damage.

Jerry's mission was simple: to alleviate his suffering.

And so, Jerry channeled his pain and became an over achiever.

He earned a degree from Queens College in New York City and ventured into publishing at CMP Media. Jerry worked hard at its publication, *InformationWeek*, including a stint as Editor.

From there he joined @Ventures, the first internet-specific venture capital firm when the internet wasn't that clear to the world, yet.

Jerry was at the cusp of Silicon Alley, which is Manhattan's version of Silicon Valley on the west coast. Both the Alley and the Valley invested in technology start-ups with the hopes of an IPO exit. Many of these companies did go public and even more did not.

Jerry navigated his way from @Ventures to Co-founder and Partner of early-stage investment venture capital fund, Flatiron Partners. Based in New York City, the firm rose to its height during the internet bubble.

While at the helm with Partner Fred Wilson, Flatiron's track record included 34 investments in 28 companies, five IPOs and 10 acquisitions. Companies like GeoCities, StarMedia, The New York Times Digital, and Alacra, were some of the firm's successes.

Jerry made *Upside* magazine's list of the 100 Most Influential People of the New Economy and was cited as one of the top venture capitalists in the country by *Forbes*.

Jerry and Fred shut Flatiron down after the dot com slowdown, which led to Jerry joining JPMP as a partner. He was successful once again with investments in companies like ProfitLogic Inc., where he also served as Director until the company was bought by Oracle.

Jerry was at the pinnacle: a high profile career rise, lots of power, plenty of money, a wife, and three kids.

"I was on top of the world on the outside, but it wasn't *my* world on the inside. Trust me, money doesn't bring happiness. Title and power don't either. I was always stressed out because I was constantly behind and needed to push forward at a frantic pace. I felt like my hair was on fire and I couldn't put it out. I was slowly dying."

Success may have led Jerry, but depression continued to plague him.

"Brad, a good friend of mine, asked me once what it would be like if I was just me? Not a label like Venture Capitalist, Father, Investor…just Jerry. That resonated with me."

Jerry knew he needed to unplug. To just say f*** it! He was worn out, vulnerable, and had more questions than answers.

———◆———

Before unplugging, and while at JPMP, Jerry was already making a slight shift toward a life of service. He just didn't realize at the time how much that would play into his ultimate path.

After 9/11, he helped launch the first Financial Recovery Fund, which gave over $10 million in recoverable grants to businesses impacted by the World Trade Center attacks. He also worked closely with New York City in the competition to host the 2012 Olympic Games, raising over $6 million toward the effort. Even though London ended up hosting, New York was a front runner. Jerry was named to *Worth*'s list of the 25 Most Generous Young Americans.

Jerry loved giving back, but he needed to give to himself, too.

Jerry left JPMP.

———◆———

Jerry went to bed a highly regarded Venture Capital Titan and woke up Jerry. Just Jerry. He was alone again, but this time, he chose to be.

"My new routine took a while to get used to."

- Wake up early
- Freak Out That I Left a Great Job
- Exercise
- Stare at Computer—Look at Emails
- Begin to Slow Down from a Lightning Speed Life
- Start Taking Vitamins to Feel Better Physically
- Sublease an Office at a Non-Profit
- Still Maintain 20 Board Seats—Unplug?
- Dress Up in Khakis and Go into Manhattan—What Am I Doing Here?
- Start to Wander…
- Work with Depression…Exhausting…Could Use a Nap

- Begin Dance Therapy—Love to Dance!
- Start Writing
- Let My Mind Think of New Possibilities
- Maybe I Should Coach Entrepreneurs?

Shifting can be sudden, or a process. Sometimes, all or part of it happens at once. Other times, it is gradual or even a combination of the two.

For Jerry, you can see the big and small steps he took that shifted him from a very external world to an internal world.

He was beginning to heal.

———◆———

Jerry read a lot during this time.

"I read about Saul on the road to Damascus."

Saul is a story in the Bible about suffering, remorse, change, purpose, and belief. It goes like this:

Acts 9 New International Version (NIV)
Saul's Conversion

Meanwhile, Saul was still breathing out murderous threats against the Lord's disciples. He went to the high priest and asked him for letters to the synagogues in Damascus, so that if he found any there who belonged to the Way, whether men or women, he might take them as prisoners to Jerusalem. As he neared Damascus on his journey, suddenly a light from heaven flashed around him. He fell to the ground and heard a voice say to him, "Saul, Saul, why do you persecute me?"

"Who are you, Lord?" Saul asked.

"I am Jesus, whom you are persecuting," he replied. "Now get up and go into the city, and you will be told what you must do."

The men traveling with Saul stood there speechless; they heard the sound but did not see anyone. Saul got up from the ground, but when he opened his eyes he could see nothing. So they led him by the hand into Damascus. For three days he was blind, and did not eat or drink anything.

In Damascus there was a disciple named Ananias. The Lord called to him in a vision, "Ananias!"

"Yes, Lord," he answered.

The Lord told him, "Go to the house of Judas on Straight Street and ask for a man from Tarsus named Saul, for he is praying. In a vision he has seen a man named Ananias come and place his hands on him to restore his sight."

"Lord," Ananias answered, "I have heard many reports about this man and all the harm he has done to your holy people in Jerusalem. And he has come here with authority from the chief priests to arrest all who call on your name."

But the Lord said to Ananias, "Go! This man is my chosen instrument to proclaim my name to the Gentiles and their kings and to the people of Israel. I will show him how much he must suffer for my name."

Then Ananias went to the house and entered it. Placing his hands on Saul, he said, "Brother Saul, the Lord—Jesus, who appeared to you on the road as you were coming here—has sent me so that you may see again and be filled with the Holy Spirit." Immediately, something like scales fell from Saul's eyes, and he could see again. He got up and was baptized, and after taking some food, he regained his strength.

Saul in Damascus and Jerusalem

Saul spent several days with the disciples in Damascus. At once he began to preach in the synagogues that Jesus is the Son of God. All those who heard him were astonished and asked, "Isn't he the man who raised havoc in Jerusalem among those who call on this name? And hasn't he come here to take them as prisoners to the chief priests?" Yet Saul grew more and more powerful and baffled the Jews living in Damascus by proving that Jesus is the Messiah.

After many days had gone by, there was a conspiracy among the Jews to kill him, but Saul learned of their plan. Day and night they kept close watch on the city gates in order to kill him. But his followers took him by night and lowered him in a basket through an opening in the wall.

When he came to Jerusalem, he tried to join the disciples, but they were all afraid of him, not believing that he really was a disciple. But Barnabas took him and brought him to the apostles. He told them how Saul on his journey had seen the Lord and that the Lord had spoken to him, and how in Damascus he had preached fearlessly in the name of Jesus. So Saul stayed with them and moved about freely in Jerusalem, speaking boldly in the name of the Lord. He talked and debated with the Hellenistic Jews, but they tried to kill him. When the believers learned of this, they took him down to Caesarea and sent him off to Tarsus.

Then the church throughout Judea, Galilee and Samaria enjoyed a time of peace and was strengthened. Living in the fear of the Lord and encouraged by the Holy Spirit, it increased in numbers.

Like Saul, Jerry understood the pressure of being a sought after entity, the remorse at having to reject companies for investment when he himself had been rejected so many times as a child, and the juxtaposition of feeling like an outcast in his own skin.

People still revered or feared Saul even though Saul changed due to his new beliefs.

Jerry wanted to change too, regardless of what society wanted or expected of him. He wanted to find his authentic self.

His new routine was helping. Jerry was slowly beginning to crawl out of the hole he had fallen into.

He went from 225 to 175 pounds.

"I read *Let Your Life Speak*, by Parker Palmer. He struggled with depression, too." Jerry identified with Parker's message of releasing himself from the darkness and making his way toward joy and fulfillment in his work and in his life. There is value in blocking out the noise and listening to one's inner voice.

Jerry had a new hope. He was ready to face his own internal turbulence.

"Buddhism resonated with me, so I decided to go to Tibet."

Jerry ended up making four trips to Tibet, founding a school, and studying intensely under his Buddhist teacher. He learned how to empty his mind, how to stand still in the forest, and open his heart in a way that connected him to others on a more meaningful level.

Jerry is part of the *Tibetan Village Project* and serves on the Board of Directors. TVP is a non-profit organization that promotes sustainable development while preserving the cultural heritage of Tibet. The organization promotes education and entrepreneurship as a vehicle to address these challenges.

Buddhism continued to make sense to Jerry in helping him deal with his own suffering. His approach to work and life was shifting toward his most exciting venture yet.

The Four Noble Truths of Buddhism:

- The Truth of Suffering
- The Truth of the Cause of Suffering
- The Truth of the End of Suffering
- The Truth of the Path that Leads to the End of Suffering

Suffering exists, whether it is physical or mental. It has a cause and it does have an end.

Jerry trained and became certified as a professional Career and Life Coach, which led to the launch of his current company, Reboot.

Reboot is a coaching company. Coaches help entrepreneurs and their teams understand and manage the fluctuations of entrepreneurship. They support company leaders in improving the growth of their companies, their performance, and their life.

"We believe that in work is the possibility of the full realization of human potential. Work does not have to destroy us. Work can be the way we achieve our fullest self."

"This is my calling. It is who I am and where I am meant to be. Helping other entrepreneurs go deep and be successful from the inside out."

Jerry and his Reboot team host intense, multi-day workshops for start-up executives. They are a cross between self-awareness therapy and practical company growth applications based on his years of experience in venture capital.

One of the philosophies that Jerry teaches during these events is the *Crucible of Leadership*. This method allows company leaders to face challenges head on (rather than hiding from them), which enables them to discover their true selves during the introspective process.

In a way, it's like facing child abuse head on, dealing with the offender, and finding strength in oneself along the way.

Reboot goes further than coaching start-up executives at workshops. They now do podcasts in order to help entrepreneurs everywhere. Reboot is growing and thriving. And Jerry is too.

In Jerry's and Reboot's words:

"It's really about the work. It's about making the work more accessible with the launch of a podcast where we can speak with people who might not otherwise be able to be coached. Or by the increase in the frequency and effectiveness of one and multi-day workshops, discussions, and what we refer to as boot camps. And through the development of tools and services that ultimately allow each of our would-be clients to help themselves and each other.

As I often say, there aren't enough elders, mentors, therapists, and coaches in the world to meet the collective need. We have to help ourselves. In the end, this is really what Reboot is all about.

It's more than a coaching company. It's a platform where we'll use the existential challenges that arise from our work lives to move more fully into our adult human selves and, thereby, somewhat and sometimes ease the pain of the vagaries of everyday life.

I often speak of my dedication to the proposition that work should be non-violent to the self, non-violent to the community, and non-violent to the planet. I didn't want to create Reboot to merely teach that belief. I wanted to create something that lives that belief. And, in doing so, live the teachings.

I owe it to my teachers, to the elders and mentors, the allies who have entered, re-entered, or exited my life to live this out. I owe it to my children to test more fully that proposition, for I want them to come into their adult lives knowing this is possible."

Jerry is thinner now and doesn't make as much money as he did as a venture capitalist. But he's tuned in, introspective, and peaceful. He trusts his inner voice, which gives him perspective and strength.

Suffering still presents itself at times, but Jerry knows that life is a journey and he is living his path as an engaged, alive participant. Best of all, he knows with certainty that he is no longer alone. He is happy in the moment.

"I'd like to go back in time and save the 38-year-old me, but I have been told by several Reboot attendees that I have saved other 38-year-olds from their potential demise, which gives me pause. To make a positive difference in the life of another, now that is worth living for."

Portions of a Recent Inspirational Blog Post Written by Jerry

August marks 20 years since Fred (Wilson) and I founded Flatiron Partners. It's been 20 years, too, since he and I came to know Brad (Feld).

Then suddenly Fred's voice brings me back. What makes his partnership at Union Square Ventures work, he says, is love. Brad quickly rushes in and they're both off again, this time riffing about love.

Tina Turner's voice comes into my head: "What's love got to do with it?" I laugh at my own joke.

But perhaps it's no joke. Perhaps there's nothing ironic about two of the most successful VCs in the country talking about love; surprising, perhaps, but not ironic.

What does love have to do with it after all?

I think of this 20-year relationship, this odd combination wherein each of us has at times paired off with the other, collaborating, growing, and challenging each other. There's a love there.

Hearing them describe their relationships with their partners, though, I hear it even more clearly. There's love in their firms as well.

Each of us has achieved this little dream. Foundry Group (Brad Feld), USV (Fred Wilson), and, yes, even Reboot (which just celebrated its second anniversary) are each partnerships where trust abounds, where colleagues are allowed to make mistakes and take missteps, and where the best of each of us is expected and the worst of us is loved, embraced, and gently held so that it can transform into a superpower.

Love isn't merely some second-hand emotion; love is the fuel that powers great organizations.

I know that's a counterintuitive notion.

Just before the last VC boot camp Brad and I hosted, I got an email from a would-be client who described Brad as "bullet-proof" because he's been so successful.

"What risk is there for him?" the emailer implicitly asked, "No one is going to fire him."

But the investors who came to that camp saw Brad demonstrate his love of the mission by bravely, vulnerably opening himself up in ways that go beyond even the openness he shows every day in life. He not only modeled the best of what an investor can be but what an adult can achieve.

Tina knows the risk: "Who needs a heart when a heart can be broken." The risk is the broken heart that comes from shattered self-esteem. What if I speak authentically and am rejected?

Over the years, I've watched my friends Brad and Fred steadfastly put themselves out there in some inchoate bid to make the dialogue just a bit better and make investing a little bit less dominated by asses who conflate meanness with toughness.

That's real love. Love of the work. Love of the mission. Love of the potential of entrepreneurship to change lives.

What's love really got to do with it, then? Everything.

I often struggle with this odd little mantle draped over my shoulders. At this time in my life, I viscerally sense the ways folks project onto me their wishes for a guru—someone who because of gray hair or the wisdom that comes through scars and my own mistakes has the answers. The most challenging aspect of that struggle is internal; it's between my ego—basking in that projection—and the better angels of my nature who know full well that whatever wisdom I have comes from having had wise teachers.

Listening to Fred and Brad talk about the ways they and their partners have built their firms on the strength of the love—the respect, the trust, the managed egos, and the forgiveness of missteps and mistakes—at their partnerships, I see even more clearly what wise teachers my old friends have been to me.

Chapter 5 Takeaways

- "The best way to overcome the inevitable loneliness of life at the top may be to connect and mindfully attend to the process that's already underway, the unconscious sharing that undergirds every relationship."
- Take the time to unplug.
- You are always on your path. The trees are never lost. Neither are you.
- Your journey to meaning in work and life has no end; it is ongoing. The key is to embrace the ride.
- Journaling is a powerful tool to self-realization.
- Believe in something—how about yourself?

PART THREE

HOW TO SHIFT

"If you do not change direction, you may end up where you are heading."
— **Lao Tzu**

Instruction

: *knowledge or information imparted*
: *the act or practice of teaching; education*

T he *how* of making a shift is difficult to get perfect right away. Why? Because it involves making concrete choices, taking action based on those choices, and keeping at it even though it is new and bumpy at times.

Do I make a radical shift or do I do it gradually?

It depends on what leads you from drift to your shift.

You may be forced to go radical. For example, you want to save your arm or your life. Then you move to gradual because it takes many surgeries and a lot of patience to get to the point where you are as functional as possible.

For others, it is more of a progression and process or struggle over time. You drift and shift along the way, many times and in different directions until you finally end up in the most perfect place, meant only for you.

The key is, regardless of how quick or methodically you shift, you cannot give up if you drift or stumble along the way or need to shift some more in order to fine-tune your path.

> *It's about commitment, focus, and determination in order to make the shift and then make it stick.*

You already know that a shift is in order and when the time is to make it. You are on your way.

Sometimes, it's easier to make the *how* formulaic; to break it down into smaller pieces.

The winners of the Nathan's Hot Dog Eating Contest each year don't eat all of the hot dogs at once, but they do methodically eat one after another as quickly as they can until they win.

I am not saying that you need to necessarily take each small step quickly, but when your shift is in motion, you will start to see signs that flow together in order for you to successfully move into the job, relationship, location, or purpose you are meant to have. Each hotdog will appear and you will need to decide if you are willing or are able to eat it.

The shift you make may be radical or just outside your norm; it doesn't matter. The key is to make the shift and continue on your path; don't go backwards. It may be scary at first, but practice breeds familiarity, and familiarity leads to comfort.

The incredible people in the next few stories found a way to take tiny steps and big steps, small movements and radical turns, in order to make their shift to who they are today—the best of themselves.

One struggled through seemingly insurmountable obstacles, life changing events, and heart wrenching setbacks, but he broke it down and started over (sometimes again and again). Another moved radically with a total turnaround of career, which led to a life of peace and happiness.

They all moved forward. Eventually, they made it through their shift while inspiring many along the way.

Through their stories, I hope that you too will be inspired to take the steps you need to make your shift happen. You can do it. You now know that you have to do it and when to do it. It's time to learn how.

Chapter 6

OVERCOMING OBSTACLES

Darren Quinn – Successful Artist, Water Adventurer, Sudden Paraplegic

D riving at night can be scary. Driving in a whiteout snowstorm can be even scarier. Skidding on black ice at night in a whiteout snowstorm… well, that can be devastating.

Darren was asleep in the passenger seat when he and his buddy hit black ice on a single lane highway. They were on their way to some epic powder skiing in the mountains of Utah.

Because his seatbelt didn't fit comfortably in the reclined position, Darren wasn't wearing it when the accident occurred.

> *"I don't remember much—probably because I was unconscious—but from what I was told, it took a long time to find me."*

The blizzard was in full force that night with swirling winds and bouts of zero visibility. Few drivers were on the road, and the ones that were didn't stop; not because they didn't care, they just couldn't see past the windshield.

Hours went by before Darren and his friend got lucky. A mother and her son were on their way home when the boy saw something dark off of the roadside.

"Mom, stop. I think that's a car."

The force of the accident ejected Darren through the windshield and over an embankment.

The car was totaled.

———◆———

Darren was air lifted to a hospital in Salt Lake City where the most serious of emergency conditions are treated. A private jet was sent by his buddy's father to get someone from Darren's family to Utah.

It wasn't looking good. A priest was called and last rights were read.

Darren's buddy was taken to the local trauma center with bruises and a few broken bones. He walked out the next day and Darren didn't see him again for four months.

> *"When I woke up in ICU several days after the accident, my world had changed. I couldn't feel my legs or my body. My arms wouldn't cooperate. I never even got to ski."*

Darren's C5 vertebrae had a lesion and 3, 4, 5, and 6 were all broken. A trachea was put in his throat so that he could breathe and then a plate was embedded into his skull with two bolts in order to stabilize him. Weights and pulleys provided traction. His left wrist was broken and fitted with metal framework and pins. He had a broken collarbone and knee and his internal injuries were significant. He was in ICU for 61 days.

It was a miracle that Darren survived.

Darren is an underdog.

He is David fighting against the Goliath of society; the establishment that says, you are not strong like us—you will not win.

If you go to Florence, Italy, to see The David at the Galleria dell' Accademia, you will be pulled in by the enormity of Michelangelo's marble statue, which stands more than 17 feet tall and weighs more than five tons.

David is made out of one piece of gargantuan marble that several artists attempted to conquer, yet could not. It wasn't until 1501 when Michelangelo, at 26 years of age, had a vision of what the stone could be and he agreed to take on the overpowering block.

Michelangelo was the laugh of the artist community. What could he do that no one had done before? How could he create one enormous sculpture, with zero room for error, or else the stone would be worthless and have to be discarded?

It was an impossible task.

But Michelangelo was an underdog. There were no expectations placed upon him, other than failure, so he had nothing to lose. The only way to look was up.

Michelangelo chipped and smoothed away at the stone for three years to complete what is now, The David, one of the most magnificent examples of art in the world; representative of the biblical story of an underdog overcoming all obstacles.

The tale of David vs. Goliath has inspired generations. It is everlasting.

On the surface, the outcome of the battle seemed unlikely. David was a shepherd boy with no armor or spears like the giant Goliath, who was so oversized that his presence alone scared away the greatest of warriors.

But David had speed and he was what was known as a slinger. A slinger is fast, accurate, calculating. A slinger outwits his opponents. More often than not, he wins. Which is what happened in the mythological tale.

Goliath says in a booming, echoing voice to David, "Come to me." Goliath wanted his enemies close so that he could crush them, but Goliath was marred down in metal and death tools, so it was much easier to have close combat, like in taekwondo, than to throw a spear across the distance of, say, a football field with any accuracy.

David, on the other hand, preferred to keep his distance, move quickly and throw Goliath off balance. Then, he took aim.

With the help of his sling, David pitched one small stone right between the eyes of Goliath and knocked him out. Then, he cut off his head.

As you take in the statue, you can't help but notice the large handed grip of the ball in his right hand and the sling lazily resting over his left shoulder. David appears relaxed, calm and even, but the intensity of his eyes combined with the protrusion of biceps, triceps, and veins tells us otherwise.

It is the calculation before the fight. The calm before the life or death storm.

When Darren woke up and discovered that he was at a disadvantage—that his body wasn't working and his speech was laborious due to spinal and neurological damage—like David, he had to rely on his wits and resolve, which were as sharp as ever. They needed to be for the fight that lay ahead.

Like David, Darren had to find a way to win or else life would crush him.

Life isn't fair—or so it often seems.

You wake up with excitement and anticipation for the day, and the next thing you know, you are stuck in bed with a body that can't move.

You talk to it, scream at it, cajole it into cooperating, but it won't. It's like a prison sentence.

But getting out of prison happens too and, after four months in the hospital, Darren was ready to be released. Although he was a paraplegic now, he was determined to conquer.

Goliath was waiting.

———◆———

Did you know that physical and mental devastation happens to men in the military every day after they do tours in the Middle East and other war torn regions? Firemen and policemen see it every day, too. These amazing warriors watch friends die, they lose limbs, they kill people even though they may not want to; they live in wheelchairs and they have dreams for years about the disruption.

Darren dreams, too. He dreams that he can walk, ski, stand up.

"In a way, sleeping is best, because I am so alive in my dreams. I am free. But, then I wake up and I consciously have to decide to take on the day."

I hope you will agree with me that Darren gets a full pass—a pass from the Goliath of societal expectations and judgments.

In a blink, Darren resided outside of the establishment that he had always adhered to, so freedom to break the rules in order to explore any and all means of moving forward in a productive way is his right. It no longer mattered what others thought. What mattered was life in a new body and what he was going to do with it now.

"I should have died that night, but I didn't.
It had to be a sign that it wasn't my time."

———◆———

Darren was born in Los Angeles; an only child to parents who divorced when he was young. His dad moved away and his mom, who gave birth to Darren in her early 20s, needed some time. So, in first grade, Darren was sent to Utah to live with his grandparents. Since his mom and grandma butted heads pretty often, his mom didn't come around much. It was better that way.

Darren loved Utah and took to skiing right away. He hit the slopes every chance he could get.

Because he and his grandparents weren't Mormon, Darren had even more free time to ski than his friends (whose lives revolved around the church). Skiing became Darren's religion.

His lean and taut physique, accompanied by windblown, walnut colored hair was the perfect combination for free dogging and doing tricks on the slopes. He preferred the fluid styles over ski racing; racing seemed so stringent.

Darren also loved the unpredictability of bumps and jumps. From there he got into skiing the trees and shoots and hiking to cornices. Making fresh powder tracks was exhilarating.

During the spring and summer, when skiing wasn't an option, Darren started watching golf on TV with his grandpa, Bobby.

"Hey Bobby, that looks like fun. I think I'd like to try that."

"That's for old guys. Stick to skiing."

Darren did continue to ski, from the first snowfall until it melted in the spring. But he started going to the driving range, too. Golf lessons soon followed and Darren got good at it.

"Skiing was my first love, but golf was a blast, too. Between the two, I could do sports year round and life was good."

Before long, and still at a young age, Darren had fine-tuned his skills and become an accomplished athlete.

<hr />

One Easter holiday during eighth grade, Darren and his grandparents took a vacation to Coronado Island off the base of San Diego. They stayed at the famous Hotel Del Coronado. It took about five minutes for the family to decide that Coronado would be a great place to move, so they looked into the local high school, bought a house, and, after eighth grade, Darren moved from the mountains to the beach.

"Golf became part of my core routine because it took too long to get to the slopes. I made varsity my freshman year, which was pretty cool. But, I still skied whenever I could."

After the accident where he spent 61 days in intensive care and two and a half months in Utah's LDS Hospital, Darren was moved to Sharp Hospital in San Diego to begin a painful rehabilitation program. Rehab extended for another two and a half months.

Eventually, he was moved back in with his grandparents in Coronado. Grandpa Bobby and Grandma Susie became his primary caregivers and his full-time family once again.

As fate would have it, Darren's dad started making regular treks from northern California to see his son. Even though Darren never really knew his dad due to the divorce, they suddenly had lots of time to get reacquainted.

His mom showed up too, but every time she would come into her parent's home, she and Grandma Susie would fight. Darren's mom didn't ever stay long, but she did start visiting with Darren's dad again.

They ended up remarrying several years later.

"I guess something good came out of my situation. My parents got back together."

Visits from friends poured in at first. High school pals who were home from college, an old girlfriend, teachers, his golf coach, even his buddy who was driving the car the night of the accident came to see Darren on a regular basis. He, of course, felt awful, but Darren forgave him right away.

"It was just one of those unlucky things that can happen in life.
He couldn't see the ice and I didn't have my seatbelt on.
I wish I could rewind the clock, but I can't blame him."

Eventually people got busy and back to their own lives. Knocks on the door dwindled and conversations faded. Darren understood. Silence became his companion and his thoughts were his counsel.

———◆———

A nurse came in most days to check Darren's vitals and bedsores. Physical therapists worked with him and reported on tiny steps of progress: an arm that lifted with jagged, random motion, a finger that could sort of grasp, legs that remained stationary other than a slight sensation here and there.

Alternative medicine was sought out, too. Acupuncture, massage, Chinese herbs—anything that might help.

Functional duties like bathing and bedpans, feeding through a tube and administering medication, fell mostly to Grandma Susie. This went on for a while.

Darren's body had shifted drastically. Now, he needed to shift his mindset in order to figure out how to move forward.

So, Darren moved in with his cousin in Huntington Beach, in the house where Darren lived as a small boy. Cousin Greg had been coming to Coronado every weekend to spend time with Darren and to learn from the nurses. He volunteered to take Darren in.

"I moved into the room where I grew up, going backwards physically and mentally. I needed to shift my outlook toward the future, whatever that might be—not get mired in the past."

Darren knew that despite his condition, he had to rely on himself now. The problem was, as much as he wanted to, he couldn't. His cousin and nurses were helpful and appreciated, but caring for Darren was a 24-hour a day commitment.

After a year Darren moved back in with his grandparents in Coronado.

———◆———

"Susie was getting older and having a hard time lifting me. Administering medication, adjusting ropes of traction, bathing, and feeding me wasn't easy, but she was committed."

Susie continued to have hope that Darren would walk again. As his wounds scarred over and the therapists challenged him, she did her best to encourage and tell him that he would get well. Darren's mobility didn't improve.

"I think it was just too much for my Grandma Susie. She tried to be positive, but I could see the weariness in her eyes."

All the love and hope for her grandson couldn't lift Susie out of despair, which she hid from everyone.

On a particularly bright and cheery day, which matched her sunny disposition, Darren's grandma gave him the tightest hug, got into her car, parked around the corner, and put a gun to her head.

"I wish it hadn't happened. I wish she didn't have to bear my pain. I wish, I wish, I wish. But wishes don't always come true, so I had to find another way to survive."

Grandpa was devastated by the news of his wife's choice and, with sordid grief, took over daily duties.

It soon proved too much for his aging body as well, and while he loved his grandson dearly, he knew that they had to come up with a new plan.

Everyone needed a break, so with the help of caretakers, Darren went to Italy for a month in May of 1990 to see if he might be able to get inspired. It was there that he created a marble statue. No, it wasn't The David, but it took David-like resolve to complete it.

Upon returning, he rented a house in Coronado and moved in with a roommate/caregiver who was also a navy seal. They lived there for five years.

Twenty-four-hour care was arranged. His cousin would visit as much as he could and his parents when they could (from Arizona where they now lived). Friends dropped by now and then; but, for the first time, Darren was truly on his own.

It was time for Darren to find a way to beat Goliath and win at life.

—————◆—————

After graduating from Coronado High School and before the accident, Darren attended the University of Utah. It was during his freshman year that he quickly realized that school was not his strength, so he went back to live with his grandparents in Coronado and figure out what he might do with his life.

It was Darren's first life shift, but not even close to the one that would change him forever.

"I was a pretty good golfer and thought about training to go pro. There was a kid ahead of me in high school who got a scholarship to Stanford and I thought I was almost as good, so I gave it a lot of thought. I also loved to ski, but I knew I wasn't as good at that. Art was always of interest…"

Darren has loved to draw since he was a kid. He drew everything from flowers to buildings, furniture to bikes; he even drew a pretty good rendition of his stubby high school math teacher.

After dropping out of college, Darren walked into the studio of famed art instructor, Monty Lewis, who happened to live in Coronado. Monty had retired from teaching at the Coronado School of Fine Arts and wasn't taking on pupils anymore, but Darren knocked on his door anyway.

Monty chewed on the end of his pipe and looked Darren up and down. Was this kid for real?

"I think he saw that I really wanted to learn and not just doodle anymore."

Darren would be the last student Monty ever taught. It was basically an apprenticeship.

"I learned to draw in several mediums under Monty's guidance. Watercolors, oils, pastels, charcoal; whatever Monty was willing to teach me."

Darren was turning into a very good artist.

—————◆—————

The next February, a particularly good snowstorm was blowing into Utah. Darren's buddy called him up and said, "Let's go!" They got as far as Provo, Utah when the accident happened.

After living on his own in Coronado for a few years, Darren began dreaming of moving to Hawaii. His navy seal roommate was also thinking about a move to Hawaii. So, along with an entourage of care, they took a few trips to the islands to see if it was even possible.

"Getting me to and from Hawaii was a huge feat.
I still couldn't do anything for myself."

Darren settled on Maui because there was a good hospital nearby. He ended up getting a place on the north shore. Round-the-clock care was still a must, but Darren loved his new home. He met many new friends on the island and had various roommates during his 15 years in Hawaii. One of them was a cute German girl who was there to windsurf. She knew all of the pros who would come over to Darren's compound to hang out. Darren wished that his friendship with the cute blond could have developed into something more, but he is a realist and was happy just to hang with her.

Another roommate was on the windsurfing World Cup Tour. He introduced Darren to one of his pals, Jacques Pauvert, who was a previous windsurfing pro and now a chef. Darren and Jacques became great friends.

One day Darren was sitting in his new friend's restaurant and the question came up:

"How can we get Q-Ball on a windsurfer?" They talked about strapping a lawn chair on a board and making sure it didn't tip over. The idea was challenging, but the possibilities were wide open.

Little did he know, but Darren was about to fulfill a lifelong dream, which took more than a village to make happen.

Through more contacts, including a famous board shaper named Richard Green, a catamaran-type windsurfer was designed and built just for Darren. It hosted a raised platform to hold the seat and run the track mast. The boat was tested and retested for stability. Pontoon boards were added and it was tested some more. It took several years to perfect Darren's ride.

And then the day came. His friend Jacques sailed the boat the entire way through the crossing from Maui to the tiny island of Molokai over crashing waves and huge swells. Two jet skis followed closely just in case. They landed on a deserted beach where a truck was waiting to take Darren to a helicopter, which transported him back to Maui. The helicopter had no doors and soared through the sky. It was another rush for Darren.

> *"I felt like I could fly across the water and the sky. I forgot I was a paraplegic."*

Darren's spirit was healing, even though his body remained in purgatory.

The high of possibility motivated him and Darren started to paint on a regular basis.

He had sold a few paintings to kind collectors before moving to Hawaii from California, but something told him it was time to get serious.

Because Darren has no finger dexterity, he wears a splint on his right hand to help him hold a paintbrush. Darren needs assistance mixing colors and turning the paper, but he is good at giving direction.

Darren also has no tricep on his right arm and basically has to draw from his shoulder and elbow. He can't push straight out, so he gains momentum and swings his shoulder, which moves his arm in one sweeping motion. It is frustrating and it takes a long time to do a painting, but, like David against Goliath, he stays the course until he wins.

When Darren messes up a brushstroke because the brush moves too far due to a lack of control of his arm movement, he simply covers his mistake with duct tape. Duct tape sticks to his hands and, with a few tries, he is able to place it onto the paper and begin again.

He beats the odds and a painting is born.

One of my favorite paintings of Darren's is the word "Amore" that he creates in different bright colors. It is painted over duct tape.

"I never thought that duct tape would be something that people would buy, but it added texture and I liked the contour on paper. I started using duct tape in all of my paintings."

Darren sold a few paintings, but it wasn't a consistent source of income.

His Grandpa Bobby moved to Hawaii to live with Darren for a year, but he felt isolated, so he moved in with Darren's parents, who had shifted from Arizona to Napa in northern California.

Bobby died a few years later while gardening and left Darren a trust fund to live on.

Todd, Darren's best friend and roommate during his year at the University of Utah, ended up marrying another friend of Darren's who also attended the school. Her name is Giada De Laurentiis. Todd and Giada moved to Los Angeles and Giada became a very good chef. So good in fact, that a TV show on the Food Network was created that featured Giada and her Italian cooking. Darren gave them his first Amore painting as a wedding gift.

When it came time to design the set for the show, Giada called Darren.

Darren's paintings of flowers, Picasso-like renditions, and "Amore" paintings were displayed for the world to see from the comfort of their living room.

Sales soared.

Giada later opened a restaurant in Las Vegas near Caesar's Palace and the Bellagio and, once again, Darren supplied some of the art to create the ambiance. Many people have bought his paintings after seeing them on the walls of the restaurant.

Darren's accident may have prevented him from becoming a professional golfer or skier, but he did become a professional artist. His life had shifted in a way he never dreamed of.

**Giada De Laurentiis on the set of the Food Network television show
with Darren's "Amore" painting in the background**

After 15 years in Hawaii, Darren's health took a turn for the worse. His lungs grew weak and he developed bladder issues, which required him to travel to UCLA for a full bladder reconstruction to remove five large bladder stones and fix damage that accumulated over the past decade. He returned to Maui four months after the surgery, but soon developed an abdominal blockage which required another surgery. Pneumonia later sprouted from air that was too moist for his aging body, and Darren was advised to retreat to a drier environment.

With his team of caregivers, Darren moved to Palm Springs.

When I went to see him at his home, it took a half hour for his caregiver to get him ready. He came out in his wheelchair with shorts and no shirt, and a tan that only years in Hawaii could perfect.

"Palm Springs makes sense for me because I am not too far from UCLA, which has one of the best hospitals around. I miss the water though."

Moving back to the mainland proved beneficial for his art, as well. Darren was the featured artist at the monthly Los Angeles Art Walk in downtown L.A. and sales increased. He put 27 pieces in Giada's new restaurant in the Cromwell hotel in Las Vegas and individual commission requests came in for pieces of certain sizes.

As for his health, with the move to a drier climate, the pneumonia cleared up, but, because of the nature of his injuries, Darren has developed further stomach issues and may need more operations. He is on medication for urology problems and deals with rotating clammy or sweaty skin on a regular basis, although a recent drug has helped reduce the swings. His bladder may need another procedure.

Regardless of his health ailments, Darren is happy and he continues to paint. He can paint huge paintings or small ones. His studio drawers are filled with them. They are all beautiful. If I could afford them all, I would own one of each.

Darren has beaten Goliath; he has won. And while there are days that he struggles more than others—and yes, he does get depressed sometimes—he continues to paint.

He paints his dreams, his love of nature, and he puts his heart on paper.

Darren has shifted to a life of meaning and purpose and has been able to spread his beautiful creations throughout the world. I am honored to know Darren and to share his story.

"I am not the man I was, but I am a new man with a lot to be thankful for."

As for the buddy who was in the accident with him? He is now a well-known chef with several restaurants of his own. He recently hosted an art show for

Darren that raised money for a high tech van that transports Darren all around Palm Springs and back and forth to UCLA whenever he needs to go. All we need to add to Darren's full life is a girlfriend!

You can watch the movie, *The Crossing*, about Darren's windsurfing adventure from Maui to Molokai, a feat never done before by someone with Darren's condition, at darrenquinn.com/videos/.

You can read more about Darren and see his art at www.darrenquinn.com.

Chapter 6 Takeaways

- Be open to the ups and downs of life. A window *will* open for you.
- You already know what you are good at. Even if you have limited resources available (including your body), pursue, pursue, pursue.
- Reach out and surround yourself with supportive people. Love does conquer all and we need love to overcome.
- If you need a break, take it. Don't push yourself to the point of exhaustion. It will get done.
- There is no such thing as impossible.
- Try not to care what others think, because others will judge you. If you have an idea, take a chance and move it forward. Rewards are waiting.
- Regardless of what capacity you may have, live your life. Don't have regrets. The clock only moves forward and so must you.

Chapter 7

FAITH BEYOND REASON

**Sloan Walsh – Woman of Faith,
Parent Education Instructor, Amazing Mother of Three**

Sloan loves to look up. She finds answers to the questions in her life as she follows billowy white cotton clouds floating across a background of deep blue.

"I see God in the sky."

Actually, Sloan sees God everywhere, in all things and in all people. She is the closest person to perfect unconditional love and acceptance that I know.

But, it wasn't always that way.

---◆---

"I had a rough childhood, lived through a broken heart, battled depression, and got very sick on more than one occasion. I had to make it through a lot to get to where I am now. Every time I thought I had made it over a hurdle, there was another obstacle to face. In the beginning, I felt that God may have forgotten about me, but something in me kept holding on and I learned how to trust Him in the midst of deep valleys," she explains.

In some ways, Sloan's life reminds me of the life of Job in the Bible.

The story goes something like this *(from Spark Notes about the Bible)*:

Job is a wealthy man with a large family and extensive flocks. He is "blameless" and "upright," always careful to avoid doing evil (1:1). One day, Satan ("the Adversary") appears before God in heaven. God boasts to Satan about Job's goodness, but Satan argues that Job is only good because God has blessed him abundantly. Satan challenges God that, if given permission to punish the man, Job will turn and curse God. God allows Satan to torment Job to test this bold claim.

In the course of one day, Job receives four messages, each bearing separate news that his livestock, servants, and ten children have all died due to marauding invaders or natural catastrophes. Job tears his clothes and shaves his head in mourning, but he still blesses God in his prayers.

Satan appears in heaven again, and God grants him another chance to test Job. This time, Job is afflicted with horrible skin sores. His wife encourages him to curse God and to give up and die, but Job refuses, struggling to accept his circumstances. Job's friends try to convince him that he has done wrong to deserve these ongoing punishments while all the time God and Satan believe him to be a righteous man. Nevertheless, he is tested, again and again.

The overall theme in the Book of Job is trying to understand why God would allow good people to suffer. Job wants to justify God's punishments and not turn against him, but he can't understand why evil people receive blessings and yet he, a good man, is punished.

Sloan was born on April 4th—the fourth child born on the fourth day of the fourth month and fourth hour in the morning exactly four years after her big sister. The number four in Biblical symbolism represents creation. On the fourth day, during God's week of creation, he created the sun, moon, and stars (Genesis 1:14-19).

Other words for creation include:

- Innovation
- Beginning
- Start
- Idea

Through every challenge Sloan would face, it was her ability to begin again that would eventually pull her through. She had no idea how many beginnings lie ahead.

Sloan's Southern California middle class family was not a religious one, but they were the right kind of societal brood that most people would be happy to be born into; at least on the outside. Sloan looked up to her two older brothers and one older sister. They were in life together.

As for her parents:

"My poor mother was simply trying to hold it all together. Three children and a volatile husband were a lot to handle. Then, I came along unplanned. Even though my mother has shared that I was special from the beginning (she describes me as being born with a star over my head), I think a fourth child may have pushed her over the edge." Sloan remembers her home life as full of stress and chaos.

———◆———

As Sloan grew, she closely observed the world around her and had a constant, itching feeling that something was missing.

"All I ever wanted was to be part of a happy family in a loving household, doing what I was passionate about, and enjoying the fruit of it."

But that wasn't Sloan's life.

She dreamed of it anyway.

"As parents, we cannot give our children that which we don't have," Sloan explains. "Our unprocessed hurts are often handed down to our children, which was surely done in my family. My father was a victim of horrific war experiences in WWII. He never spoke of it, but our family experienced his pain when he acted out hidden rage and fear."

Sloan's home environment was volatile and uncertain at times. Although her mother did the best she could, she had minimal support.

"My mother's own childhood was tough, too. Sometimes life repeats itself."

Were all of your memories of your father unpleasant? I asked her gently.

"I do have pleasant memories of sitting on my dad's lap as a child, taking walks together under the stars, and listening to him talk of his love for our country. At that time, I lived to make him proud of me and dreamed of doing something so great that it would measure up to his sacrifices." She smiled at the thought of the quieter, reflective shared times.

"Sadly, though, as I saw his emotions unleashed on all of us again and again, especially my mother and brothers, I came to disdain him. I was disappointed in my hero."

In spite of her conflicting emotions, Sloan assigns credit to good memories from her childhood, too.

"My mother tried hard to make holidays really special and we also did a lot of camping. The whole family would pile into our blue Chrysler Imperial that pulled a large trailer along behind. One summer we went all over the United

States, stopping along the way at various campsites to enjoy the local town and scenery. But, the car broke down a lot. When it did, my brother's would hitchhike to the nearest town to get a tow truck. I can't imagine how terrified my mother was wondering if her boys would return."

Sloan loved long summers, running around barefoot and swimming in the pool on the military base where she grew up in the middle of the Mojave Desert.

Her favorite times were with her many close friends. She practically lived over at their houses and became somewhat of an adopted daughter to many kind families. She cherished her lifelong best friend who, although in many ways the opposite of her, shared so many fun times together. She was the one to introduce Sloan to what it meant to have a relationship with God.

Due to overall conditions at home, Sloan began dealing with depression in her teen years. While we all get depressed at times, Sloan had a hard time shaking hers. Life felt hopeless. Her family was unable to provide emotional support and, later on, the love of her life broke her heart, leaving her to feel that she had nowhere to turn.

According to Dr. Carol Glod with *Families for Depression Awareness*, depression is greater in teens than children. Two and a half percent of kids 6-12 years old suffer from depression and eight percent of teens develop depression. Some studies show that the percentage could be as high as 20 percent for teens with depression.

Compared to boys, girls tend to experience higher degrees of depression past the age of 12. Often, it goes undiagnosed.

There had to be a way out of the downward spiral. Sloan began looking for answers outside of her present world.

Her sister and her best friend had become Christians when Sloan was young and slowly she began to see through their experiences that there might be a greater hope to draw upon in life.

Sloan wanted and needed hope.

With hope and curiosity as her guides, Sloan occasionally joined different Christian organizations, all of which had a positive impact on her. Her best friend was a steady force and influence on Sloan as she navigated her way through what God was all about.

———◆———

After high school, Sloan attended The University of California at Santa Barbara. She was still dealing with a devastating breakup, and spent the early morning hours before class sitting on a bluff, looking at the sky, and listening to the ocean.

As a natural progression, she began to guide questions about life to God. Months of daily meditation ensued and Sloan began to hear back from God within. She felt her heart slowly begin to heal.

Sloan eventually concluded that there *was* a Father figure, albeit a heavenly one, that loved her no matter what.

She would need this strength of belief.

"Sometimes I would pray and wait on God for so long that I would miss my early classes."

"I was trying to get over my depression and broken heart and to figure out how to be happy in life."

"I actually believe the practice of prayer changed my brain structure. There is science now to support this."

According to *Studies of Advanced Stages of Meditation in the Tibetan Buddhist and Vedic Traditions—a Comparison of General Changes* by Alex Hankey:

A study was done on advanced practices of Tibetan Buddhist meditation in remote regions of the Himalayas, with established results on long-term practitioners of the Transcendental Meditation programs.

Many parallel levels of improvement were found, in sensory acuity, perceptual style and cognitive function, indicating stabilization of aspects of attentional awareness. Together, with observed increases in EEG coherence and aspects of brain function, such changes are consistent with growth towards a state of total brain functioning, i.e. development of full mental potential.

In other words, lots of praying is advantageous to your health and mental state. You evolve.

Sloan states; "The practice of prayer completely changed my life. Not only did it actually help me process and heal, I came into contact with a powerful God who revealed Himself to me in unbelievable ways."

———◆———

College was a time of real growth for Sloan, with drifting and shifting throughout the four years.

Sloan changed her major a number of times, searching for the right path for her future. Her father became impatient and urged her to consider teaching, which wasn't her first choice. Little did she know it would end up being her life's calling and her passion.

She joined a sorority where she met some of her dearest friends, but faced many challenges navigating her studies, social life, and her Christian faith.

"As an introvert, it was a shock for me to live with so many outgoing, vivacious, and sometimes wild girls! I'm not sure how well I fit in sometimes."

Sloan was becoming more devoted to God and his guidance, and struggled to live her faith in the open. The college atmosphere was not built around faith. Parties maybe, but not faith.

"I was part of a pretty strict religious community during college. Looking back, I don't know how healthy it was. I found myself judging everyone and setting a high standard of living for myself and others. I think it was probably due to my unstable background. I found so much security in rigid Christianity and sadly it was not very life giving. I did, however, make lifelong friends during those years and see that those experiences taught me a lot about life and growing up."

The challenges that Sloan would face later in life would bring her to a greater understanding of God's love and goodness in contrast to the powerlessness of a rigid religious mindset.

———◆———

Even though, outwardly, Sloan was doing all the right things as a Christian; inwardly, depression lingered and the self-imposed expectation of perfectionism was an ever present companion.

Additionally, an ongoing battle of obsessive exercise and minimal eating plagued her. She continued to self loathe no matter how thin she became.

Perfection can be taxing on anyone, and the discontent for not achieving it can play havoc with the mind and emotions. Sadly, for Sloan, the quest for the perfect body led to an eating disorder which would contribute to future physical and emotional challenges.

———◦———

An abstract on the link between depression and physical symptoms was published by Doctor Madjukar Trivedi in *The National Center for Biotechnology Information Primary Care Companion to the Journal of Clinical Psychiatry*. In it he reveals that:

Physical symptoms are common in major depression and may lead to chronic pain and complicate treatment. Symptoms associated with depression include joint pain, limb pain, back pain, gastrointestinal problems, fatigue, psychomotor activity changes, and appetite changes.

———◦———

After graduating from college, Sloan ended up becoming a teacher, just like her father wanted. She taught third grade in Los Angeles's inner city, where students spoke only Spanish. Sloan had to adapt and ended up obtaining her bilingual credential.

"In a way, I was working through my own painful childhood by pouring myself into my students and their tremendous needs. I devoted myself to them. I listened to them, tried to inspire them and let them know that they mattered. I was healing my own life as I served them, with the comfort of having God there with me."

But God's plan for Sloan went beyond helping and healing. Sloan was about to be tested in ways she never could have envisioned and surely did not deserve. The life of *Job* was coming to her doorstep and it wasn't going to be easy.

"A few years after college, I met and married a wonderful, solid man who was a true kindred spirit. We had such an instant bond I knew when I first met him that we had a future together."

> *"Shortly after getting married, I came down with the flu. At first, I didn't think it was a big deal, but it wouldn't go away."*

Sloan's flu began with a high fever that kept her in bed for days, and when she was finally well enough to go back to work, her strength was weak and daily tasks became laborious. The intense fatigue reached deep into her bones.

"I had swollen glands and a low-grade fever pretty much all of the time. It was frightening to be sick and not have any answers from the doctors I was seeing. I began to pray for healing."

Sloan quit work and focused on getting well. She was diagnosed with chronic fatigue syndrome, an autoimmune disease.

Sloan has always wondered if the stress of her childhood and her eating disorder had taken its toll on her body.

> *It took five years for her to recover.*

During recovery, Sloan learned a lot about self-care, rest, good nutrition, the power of creativity, and prayer. Her husband was a source of great comfort and support. Not only was her body healing, but her soul was as well.

During rest and regeneration, for the first time, Sloan had freedom to dream. She dreamed of creating.

Whether it was a future curriculum, a painting, a quilt for a friend's new baby, a scrapbook, or writing in her journal, she found creating to be a life force that flowed through her and helped her to finally get out of bed. Creating also became a healing antidote to the dark cloud of depression that plagued her since childhood.

Prayer continued to become a bigger part of Sloan's life. She spent hours in devotion each day as she tended to her health. Life was being restored.

As Sloan's strength grew, hopes for her own future grew too.

She loved welcoming friend's new babies into the world with homemade gifts and her presence. She waited outside the delivery room with smiles of joy for so many.

Maybe a baby would be in her future.

But, like *Job*, God had more challenges in store for Sloan.

As hard as she and her husband tried, Sloan could not get pregnant. Devastation set in once again and feelings of confusion, anger, and vulnerability arose.

"Gatherings became tough. Friends would surprise everyone with an announcement of a baby coming, without realizing how painful it all was for us. We were constantly being asked when we were going to have kids."

On occasion Sloan would burst into tears and need to leave the room. She became pretty bitter and felt judged and misunderstood by many friends and family members which caused her to withdraw. Not being able to get pregnant was a huge obstacle to her faith.

Regardless of where she stood with God at the time, Sloan and her husband refused to accept defeat. They met with doctor after doctor, underwent surgeries and suffered through numerous fertility procedures.

For eight years, Sloan and her husband desperately tried to start a family.

Nothing worked.

In order to cope with the disappointment, Sloan threw herself back into teaching. Anything to get her mind off what she wanted most.

She devoted herself to the lives of her students, which at times was very difficult because Sloan was plagued with the possibility that she might never have a child of her own.

———◆———

Along the way, something shifted inside her. Sloan began to love her work. She became passionate about learning new strategies for teaching her students to read. She knew that she was making a difference in other's lives and it became fulfilling on its own.

Not long after getting back to teaching, Sloan became trained as a literacy specialist and started training teachers in an early literacy program that had recently been implemented in her school district. She was a natural.

Her training and success led to opportunities where she would speak at teaching conferences and train future teachers at local universities. Sloan was voted *Teacher of the Year* and even had some of her work published.

She became grateful to God for helping her find her passion and turned her attention back to him.

> *When we give unconditionally from a place of passion and joy,*
> *it is amazing how much good comes our way.*

Even so, in spite of her success, Sloan still desperately wanted a family. It was a dream since childhood. The years were rapidly passing and the aching desire in her heart increased exponentially.

One may question why a woman of devoted prayer would face so many unanswered petitions. But, Sloan claims that these years of…

> *…seeking God in earnest built in her a muscle of faith*
> *that she would have never had if she hadn't suffered.*

Sloan came to know God on a more real and personal level; he became her source of healing and renewal through years of yearning.

Sloan learned patience.

Adoption entered the conversation with her husband, but all of the books and articles that Sloan read on the subject were discouraging.

Yet, God works in mysterious ways...

One weekend while her husband was out of town, a friend invited Sloan to an adoption seminar. She didn't want to go, but after some encouragement she relented. Sloan sat in the back of the room with arms folded tightly across her chest and a permanent scowl on her brow.

While she was there, however, something unexpectedly caught her attention.

During a short break, the presenter put up a video of two and three-year-old children in a Russian orphanage. Her deadened heart started beating again. Feelings of joy and passion, not unlike the gates of heaven opening, filled her entire being and she knew.

"We were going to adopt. I was sure of it. It was as though God was showing me my calling."

Sloan and her husband began the long, arduous process of international adoption.

They were quickly dismayed to discover that the adoption agency they were working with only placed older children, and they wanted a baby. They considered a domestic adoption, but at every turn, something didn't pan out and it left her depressed and unmotivated to move forward. She and her husband were at their wits end and not getting along. Sloan was ready to give up.

The Winter Olympics were on television one evening and while Sloan was enjoying watching the Russian ice skaters, she sensed God speaking to her.

"I recalled that the only time I felt joy about adopting was when I saw that video of the Russian orphanage."

Sloan began to cry and called a friend familiar with the process. The friend validated Sloan's premonition and encouraged her to try again.

The next morning, Sloan called the adoption agency and found out that they were now working with a baby house in St. Petersburg, Russia.

The journey to bringing their first son home began.

"I had been feeling so sorry for myself that I didn't even see the signs. God was bringing me back to him and preparing me for my true purpose all along."

Pay attention to the signs.

Small miracles began to happen.

On one occasion when she and her husband were preparing to start the adoption paperwork, Sloan walked across the room and felt that she heard God's audible voice.

"I heard the words, 'Child of the Promise.'"

The quote sounded unusual, so Sloan grabbed her Bible and began looking for scripture that spoke to the message. She found a passage in the Book of Romans in the Bible that says, "It's not the natural child who is God's child, but the child of the promise."

"I felt that God was telling me that He was giving me the child He had promised me."

And then the doves came.

"We started getting these amazing visits from doves. They would fly into our yard and coo. One time my husband was walking out to his car and a white dove was sitting on the driver side mirror. He stared at him and the dove calmly looked right back. We had another come and just look at us through the window. We started seeing flocks of doves flying over us on the freeway or settling in around our home."

On one of their adoption visits to Russia, they saw several billboard advertisements with people releasing doves. As they entered the orphanage, paper white doves were plastered all over the walls.

It was as though God knew he needed to send Sloan a constant concrete confirmation that they were on the path that he had set. Sloan was excited and scared and confident and insecure all at the same time.

"When I held our baby in my arms, I was so overwhelmed by all it took to get to this moment, I thought I might actually get sick, which is not the reaction

I expected. But as soon as I focused on looking into my child's eyes, all pain, fear, and uncertainty melted away. I was a mother now."

Sometimes when we shift, we have to work through a lot of pain in order to clear out the past and move forward toward what we are meant to do and be. We need to *let go and let God* as we often hear, or just simply stop trying to control or fix. Going with the flow, even when it's not exactly how we want it to be, can be difficult; yet, in the end, things do happen as they should.

Sloan had a lot to work through in her life—a tough upbringing, depression, sickness, infertility—and she had to rid her emotional self of the old in order to bring in the new.

God was preparing her for her core purpose: to be the best mom possible.

But parenting a child who had spent his first few months in an orphanage was not easy.

"It was definitely all about healing and restoring my child from early trauma and abandonment. He would let out huge cries, as though he was crying for his birth mother or grieving the pain of neglect. The initial days were an adjustment. I would hold, rock, soothe, and comfort for long hours at a time. I'd spend hours praying for healing and restoration over my son's little spirit."

It worked.

Sloan had no idea how to be a good mom, but maybe God did. She felt Him speak to her often and give her the answers she needed in order to do the right thing. She didn't want her son to have a childhood like hers, so she did all she could to learn the best parenting methods possible. She was going to raise her son in a way quite unlike her own experience.

Sloan learned about 'attachment parenting' and read every book she could on the subject.

"I had the good fortune of meeting Dr. Tina Payne Bryson who had trained under Dr. Daniel Siegel at the Mindsight Institute at UCLA. Dr. Siegel was the author of my favorite parenting book, *Parenting from the Inside Out*. I learned about the latest brain research and how the emerging field of interpersonal neurobiology related to parenting."

In his book, Dr. Siegel explains the concept of implicit memory [early in the womb and in the body before the brain is developed] and explicit memory [the memory we can recall] which helped Sloan understand how to help her son process early trauma.

Dr. Payne Bryson was writing a parenting book with Dr. Siegel. Sloan had the opportunity to attend her classes and learn directly as to the best approaches to parenting.

Sloan started praying for her son to heal from implicit memory due to stress in the womb, fear of abandonment, and anxiety at feeding time while at the orphanage.

When her son's emotions ran high, Sloan soothed him, rather than punishing or reprimanding him, and calmed him down with soft words of encouragement. Her desire was to teach him self-regulation as a way to develop emotional intelligence.

Sloan also went to *Mommy and Me* parenting classes at a local church where she met and enjoyed time with other new moms. Shortly after, she was asked to join the staff to teach the classes for mothers of toddlers. Inside she felt it was a bit ironic that she would now be teaching moms after her long journey to parenthood; but, once again, God had other plans.

Sloan overcame her insecurities and settled in as a parenting teacher, which led to teaching even more parenting classes. Sloan has been teaching about parenting for more than 15 years.

Sloan and her husband adopted their second child and she continued to develop her mothering skills and style, all based on love. Their second son had challenges too. He needed a lot of intervention, and so Sloan once again poured herself into learning new and innovative ways that would help to raise him. Everything she learned that worked, she would teach to other new parents.

"I read every parenting book I could and I prayed a lot. I eventually developed my own philosophy on parenting that I now use in all of my classes and seminars."

But the hurdles weren't over for Sloan.

In February of 2006, when her sons were 8 and 6, Sloan noticed a lump pressing against the underwire of her bra. She ignored it for a while.

When she finally went to the doctor for a mammogram test a few months later, he knew right away that Sloan had breast cancer.

Sloan's world was turned upside down yet again, but she also knew that God had healed her in many ways in the past. Sloan desperately wanted to believe that God was with her and would walk her through this new gauntlet.

"He just couldn't abandon me now!"

Little did Sloan know, but a baby girl was being born at the same time on the other side of the world.

Sloan's support system during her fight against breast cancer was overflowing. She was grateful for the rides, the food, the visits, and the love. Her best friend since childhood, the one who she relied on through everything, never left her side. It seemed as though the entire universe was rooting for her to heal.

During chemotherapy treatments, Sloan would pray for others and thank God for all He had given her. She was entering yet another shift; a shift in attitude toward her physical plight. Instead of confusion, she only had gratitude for all God had given her. Sloan believes that God healed her. Ten years later, she is grateful for her healthy life.

A few months after cancer treatments, during a church service where prayers were being offered for children, a woman she did not know approached her and said, "Three months." Sloan had no idea what the woman meant. The woman was referring to a miracle that would happen within that time frame. Sloan began to pray for another child and exactly three months later, Sloan and her husband were referred a baby girl who would be their daughter.

Their dream of adding to their family was coming true. The process of adopting their daughter was one of the most miraculous of all.

With a bald head and still on heavy cancer medications, Sloan and her husband traveled to the remote country of Kyrgyzstan in Central Asia and completed an international adoption. The process ran smoothly and was over in just a few months. They overcame unbelievable odds to bring her home.

The doves were there all along, cooing them on.

———◆———

Life felt good despite the cancer, and Sloan began to see her prayers being answered. She grew in health and faith and was truly happy with her wonderful family that God had designed.

Her parenting classes were hugely successful and she enjoyed a nice balance between work and family. Gratitude permeated all that she did and she knew that everything she had was a gift.

Sadly, again, a few years later, there was yet another challenge for Sloan to face. In a way, it was the toughest one of all.

"My husband Bob has always been my rock. He is truly my best friend in the world. We have been very fortunate to have a solid marriage."

Nine years after Sloan battled breast cancer, when the kids were 15, 14, and 8, they were given the grave news that Bob had bladder cancer. Another devastating surprise.

Sloan thought that all of her trials were over, but God must have seen enormous strength in her to face cancer yet again.

Her husband endured numerous surgeries and challenges and during the ordeal Sloan found herself relying heavily on God to carry her through.

"Things got pretty dire, and I thought I might lose him forever. He underwent treatments and various surgeries from some amazing doctors, which, thankfully, combined with God's healing, saved his life. During it all, my love for my husband was never greater. I worked tirelessly from sun up to sun down to hold everything together and am thankful every day for his recovery."

———◆———

As for Sloan, presently she is healthy, her children are thriving, her husband is well, she is a highly respected and sought after Parent Educator and is truly the essence of love.

She has been tested and terrified. She has shifted several times to become the person she is meant to be: a great mom, an inspirational teacher, and a loving, selfless person.

When asked what was the most special way you've shown someone you love them, Sloan replied, "Helping my children heal from the early trauma of abandonment and neglect and also caring for my husband when he had cancer."

When asked what was the most special way you've been shown that you are loved? "God's tangible presence in my life and the care I received when I had cancer."

And remember the doves that appeared before and during each of their adoptions? Well, they still visit all of the time.

Chapter 7 Takeaways

- Even if you don't understand, know that there is a perfect plan for you. Pay attention to the signs; they are always there.
- Leave your ego at the door and see what great things can happen.
- Be open to changing your perspective when things aren't going your way. We are not always right.
- Love, love, love. In all that you do, love.
- Treasure the special moments; they add up to a fulfilling life.
- Prayer can heal you. Try it.
- We teach best what we most need to learn.
- It's okay to be an introvert and contemplative in an extrovert world.
- When you look back, it all adds up perfectly.
- Gratitude is the key to happiness.
- Sometimes we suffer, often. Rise above it.
- Trust.

Chapter 8
SYNCHRONICITY

**Manoj Chalam (and his wife, Jyothi), Ph.D., Chemical
Engineering, Hindu Deity Art Collector, Co-Founder of Unique
Arts & Vivekodayam, Teacher of Hindu and Buddhist Archetypes**

M anoj meets more than 30,000 people around the world every year at yoga workshops, wellness retreats, and self-realization festivals. He is invited to teach about happiness, enlightenment, simplicity, and trusting the journey. His message is transformative.

But Manoj had to transform himself first.

How did he do it? By paying attention to the signs along the way.

———◆———

"We are all heroes and we are living a hero's journey," Manoj explains as a key component to his philosophy, which is a little Carl Jung and a lot Hindu deity.

What he means by this is that everyone on the planet has dreams and aspirations as well as obstacles to overcome. We wish to be the hero of our own lives; we want to realize our potential, be our authentic self, and share that with the world.

How do we do this? How do we become the hero of our own lives?

If Manoj had his way, everyone would just chill out and go with the flow. Not in an idle, do nothing way, but in a way that says, *I am where I should be right now on my path in life; I don't have to stress about it; I can enjoy the journey as I look for the signs that will propel me forward.*

> **"Look, we are all going to die, that is a fact.**
> **The real question is how are we living now?"**

This question is at the core of Manoj's teachings.

———◆———

As a child, Manoj loved tennis and table tennis. He practiced hard.

"Work ethic is important in India and I worked hard at my sports." So hard that Manoj became a 4.5 level tennis player and played at the NCAA level in ping pong. He practiced table tennis three to four hours every day and, through that discipline, learned about focus and competition. He was preparing himself for the world of business without even knowing it.

"I grew up in Mumbai and got into the Indian Institute of Technology (IIT), one of the best engineering colleges in the world. It was like MIT." He surmised that about one percent of people who write the entrance exam get in.

After IIT, the track was to go to graduate school (the best one possible) in the United States via a scholarship. For Manoj, Cornell made the most sense.

Many alumni of India's IIT colleges, after graduating from U.S. business schools, built several Silicon Valley companies. For example, graduates like Vinod Dham created the Pentium Chip. Kanwal Rekhi and Vinod Khosla co-founded Excelan and Sun Microsystems.

According to an article in the Wall Street Journal entitled "Why America's Top Technology Jobs Are Going to Indian Executives," such as Google CEO Sundar Pichai, Microsoft CEO Satya Nadella (who helped convince Silicon Valley to like Microsoft again), and Adobe CEO Shantanu Narayen, it all has to do with leadership traits.

According to Manoj, the unspoken expectation within the culture of India is be humble, to listen, and to get along with everyone. Humility is a character trait that is valued. Aggressiveness is not celebrated.

He continues that in India, the emphasis is on success in a non-socialist regime. The freedom to create is exciting and citizens are driven. And as India has become a wealthier society, the educational track has shifted to pursuing a U.S. based undergraduate education as well.

"We were like sheep then though. We did what our culture mandated. Get a good job, get married, buy a three or four-bedroom house, have kids. Get settled. It was the definition of success."

Armed with a PhD in chemical engineering (with a physics bent) from Cornell, Manoj reveled in the knowledge he had gained for the sheer love of learning. And, even though the physics emphasis within chemical engineering wasn't directly applicable to the tech world, opportunities opened for Manoj.

————◆————

But Manoj was more of a free thinker, he didn't want to be a sheep who followed the crowd. As a byproduct of his independence, he didn't fare so well inside stringent corporate environments.

*While Manoj was set up to achieve the
India dream, it was not his dream.*

Still, he went along.

Manoj worked for three companies in research development: Mobile Oil, General Electric, and Axcon. He spent about nine years in corporate America, all the while fantasizing about being a highly sought after tech executive. He built castles in his mind of being like Vinod Khosla of Khosla Ventures. His castles were made of IPOs, enormous wealth, and fame.

"Ego can be a strong force that gives one a sense of control, even though humility is supposed to be the guide."

Maybe becoming an entrepreneur would help Manoj find his place in the working world, a shift that would lead to happiness. So, he started consulting for top organizations.

Strategic technology consulting eventually led to his position as the CEO of a software company with 100 employees. He refashioned it into a start-up structure, which was lean and hungry and on the cutting edge.

Manoj had regular dealings with the venture and investment communities as the company grew. While the castle dreams continued, he was a realist and knew that the company wasn't close to that.

"I let myself get seduced by money and power. An angel investor gave us a million dollars and I dreamed of being the next IT technology darling of the industry."

Here he was, finally, in what could be considered the perfect job in the perfect industry in the perfect location at the perfect time. His family was proud.

But, life has a way of showing up.

"Then I got fired."

Manoj was suddenly faced with failure, a condition he didn't expect would affect him as strongly as it did.

"I kept getting beat up in life. It wasn't fun." So he went back to what he could control. He started consulting again.

Manoj was making money, had a wonderful wife who loved him, and they started a family. Everything seemed to be back on track; but at 38, Manoj was still unhappy.

On the one hand, he was successful as a consultant, which still sort of fulfilled a societal standard (probably because he also had a house, a wife, and a child). He looked settled on the outside.

However, on the inside, he wanted to feel more of what his wife Jyothi felt every day. Peace and happiness. He wanted to explore his inner self—his spiritual side.

"I took stock of my life. While there was comfort with my material, worldly, and executive success, it never led to happiness. Even when things worked out, happiness was only temporary."

Manoj asked himself why he was on a treadmill to nowhere and, more importantly, could he find a way to get off and find happiness some other way?

Manoj became restless.

"I used to be such a planner. Join companies, run one, get fired, consult, maybe start another company. I still wanted to be in control. Now, I was trying to control where it would be that I would find my happiness."

During this reflective time, Manoj observed his wife's behavior more closely.

He admired her daily dedication to hours of meditation and her effortlessness at being in a state of joy, regardless of circumstance.

"While I loved the tech industry, despite the ups and down, I found myself being drawn in a more spiritual direction. My wife seemed to have captured happiness on her spiritual path. I wanted that, too."

And so Manoj began to meditate and go to yoga. Not a lot at first, but as the peacefulness of the silence and stretching postures soothed him, his mind became clearer and he started to relax. He was less worried about what came next.

He read *Autobiography of a Yogi* and studied Paramahansa Yogananda. He was influenced by spiritual leaders like Deepak Chopra and started following the philosophies of Carl Jung and Joseph Campbell.

Manoj was on a quest to find real meaning and happiness in work and in his inner soul.

———◆———

"My wife talked about starting a company that collected deity art. She was spiritual from an early age and she felt a calling. I was intrigued."

Shiva: The Old is Destroyed to Make Room for the New

Manoj bought their first Hindu deity statue and set out to understand its significance.

He learned that Hindu deities are Gods to some and, while he doesn't discount their Godlike value, from his perspective, "Deities are archetypes and we all have an archetype. The first step is to understand your archetype, which will give you knowledge as to your core characteristics and strengths as you seek out your place in the world."

He didn't stop at one statue. Manoj learned about all of the Hindu and Buddhist deities and began collecting many renditions. He thought of it as a helping hobby of sorts, but one he and his wife found fascinating.

Manoj scoured flea markets, temples, and stores that sold artifacts from India. The focus became on collecting. Their accumulation expanded by importing more likenesses and making regular trips to India.

"I just wanted to help her. I found myself on a trip around the world and ended up with an entire container of deity statues. I didn't expect it. I didn't know what we would do with them. I was planning to form another start-up, but the whole spirituality path drew me in."

Before long, Manoj and Jyothi became the largest collectors of Hindu deity art in the United States.

"I got stopped at airport security a lot. Shipping the heavy metal figures cost so much that I would check in a suitcase full and then bring one on the plane with me. I got stronger because they weighed a ton. I must have looked pretty odd dragging my container through the airport. I can imagine, with my tanned skin, what people must have thought."

———◆———

Still, Manoj was in the mindset of just helping his wife with her interests until something happened that caused him to make a major shift in his own life.

"When you trust the guidance of your archetype to reach toward a state of awakening in your inner spirit, you will have the key to unlock a successful journey in work and in life."

Manoj had an inkling that he was being guided, so off to India he went again.

He visited 40 temples in 30 days.

The goal of visiting 40 temples in 30 days was part of a spiritual journey that he wanted to experience.

On the business side, he also was open to continuing to buy, acquire, and collect more deity art. Manoj wasn't sure what they were going to do with this growing mass of inspired metal, but his instincts told him that he needed to keep going.

Rather than taking a train or trying to navigate his own way around India, Manoj rented a car (which comes with a driver due to the congestion and roads that don't always make sense). The driver took him to the temples, which were primarily in distant, rural villages throughout southern India. Even though Manoj was competing with no one but himself, his work ethic was hard to mollify. He had a desire to see them all and also to collect what he could.

"I was so tired toward the end of the trip that I fell asleep in the back of the sedan. One of the deities must have been looking out for me because as soon as we were about to pass the sign for Tamil Nadu, which hosts the famous temple, Vaitheeswaran Koil, I woke up.

Vaitheeswaran Koil is the most treasured temple. It is known as the temple of Shiva the healer.

"The temple was tall and intimidating. I knew experiencing the temple wasn't as much about my life as it was about the spiritual path. Truths might be revealed."

Manoj was open to buying art from the temple if available, but, more importantly, it was where he was to have his Nadi scrolls read.

Vaitheeswaran Koil

"Ideas don't really change people; events do. T
he Nadi Scrolls were my event."

Nadi scrolls (or palm leaves)
Photo Credit: Mr. Think tank/ Flickr/CC BY 2.0>>

The Nadi scrolls are comprised of thousands of scrolls that are believed to represent the past, present, and future of all human lives as foreseen by Hindu sages in ancient times. They are known for being inspired by the Hindu deities themselves.

The viewpoint is that if you go to have your scrolls (sometimes called palm leaves) read, then you are probably supposed to. It is believed that a particular scroll has been waiting to communicate to you maybe for as long as many thousands of years.

"Turn here," Manoj called out as they passed the sign.

The driver did an illegal U-turn and they were off, bouncing in and out of traffic on lanes that didn't exist.

———◉———

Manoj was nervous and excited. Would a scroll know him? Could it tell him his future? Could it heal his soul?

"I had heard about a certain reader of the scrolls who was supposed to be very accurate. So I walked into the impressive temple and waited patiently to be seen by this keeper of the scrolls."

Before your scrolls are read, men provide a right thumbprint and women a left thumbprint. This is your unique marking unlike anyone else on the planet and, supposedly, contains the karmic backpack you have when you come into the world.

"There are 108 ways your karma can guide you in life. The Nadi scroll reader can tell you which way your path has taken and where you are going."

———◆———

The sage opened the first scroll.

"I would like to make it clear that he didn't know anything about me. The process is simple: he asks many questions and my job is to answer 'yes' or 'no.' Eventually, I am supposed to come face to face with my personal scroll that will know all about me; my past, my present, and, if I want to know it, my future."

"Your name is Pakash."

"No."

"Your mother's name is Radha."

"No."

The yes/no questioning went on for close to four hours. Lots of 'no', an occasional 'yes.'

Then it started to get really hot. No air conditioning in the thick heat. Manoj began to doubt.

"I figured that it was just a big con, kind of like the game 20 questions. If they ask me enough, they'll get to some sort of answer that resonates."

Manoj joked about the card game in the movie *Inglorious Bastards,* where Brad Pitt and his team are nervously sitting around a table in a pub with a bunch of Nazi Germans. One by one they hold cards to their forehead while the others give yes/no answers to the questions the person holding the card asks in an effort to name what is on the card. Sort of the idea.

———◆———

"And then he pulled out a scroll that would shift me forever."

"Your Name is Manoj Chalam."

Manoj was sure the reader must have gotten his name from the hotel where Manoj was staying.

"Yes."

"You were born 12 May, 1962." The hotel didn't have that information.

"Yes."

"Your mother's name is Raja Lakshmi." Manoj's draw dropped.

"Yes."

"Your father's name is Venkata Chalam."

"Yes."

Manoj was blown away.

The reader went on to tell him that he was a collector of spiritual art and that he would build a temple with the collection. He also told Manoj that he would be a teacher with a great following.

"Do you want to know the date and time that you will die?"

"Sure, I mean, yes."

"It will be on the fourth Friday on 00/00/0000 at 00:00:00."

While Manoj did not share with me the exact date and time, he did say it was comfortably in the future.

Manoj was sure that the reader could not have gotten the detailed and quantity of correct information (much of which is not included in this book) without being a psychic or having been influenced by a higher power.

Exhausted and exhilarated, Manoj knew that his life was forever changed.

———◆———

Manoj later developed yearnings, one of which was to move toward teaching. He felt called to teach about Hindu and Buddhist deity archetypes.

He drank his last beer, had his last bite of meat and went deep.

"I contacted the guru I had been working with when I started down my spiritual path and committed to an immersion."

Basically, Manoj dropped everything, went to India, and stayed with the guru in order to study and learn as much as he could.

"It was like I was dumped into water and was gasping for air. I needed to be awakened."

And he was.

Manoj learned a great deal about himself, spirituality, meditation, and practices like Vedanta, which means knowledge and end. His wife already practiced this form of yoga and meditation.

He emerged from his sojourn a new man, realizing that there is a flow in life that orchestrates everything. Maybe we don't have as much free will as we thought...

Manoj did go on to build a local temple where people can come to see the many Hindu and Buddhist deity statues that he and his wife have collected. He is holding a spiritual retreat there soon.

"The power of love will always win over the love of power."

"I never did do another start-up. I had found my purpose, my path, my meaning, and my happiness. I was a teacher, a guide, and an ever-evolving person on a spiritual journey."

Manoj believes that when a person makes a major professional shift, they should do so in a way that is in the service of others. The focus should not be on the material anymore.

His shift to teaching about Hindu archetypes has been the most fulfilling role he has ever had. It is where his true meaning lies.

Let's look at that.

Bill Gates is a good example. He founded, led, and grew Microsoft into one of the most successful companies in the world. When he was ready to move on, he and his wife created the Bill and Melinda Gates Foundation. They are committing most of their wealth to service, such as funding worldwide delivery and application of the polio vaccine, with the hopes of eradicating polio. Their global message is *all lives have equal value.*

Many wealthy entrepreneurs have pledged the bulk of their wealth to service of the greater good as well.

The Giving Pledge is a public commitment of the world's wealthiest to pledge most of their money to charity. It has attracted billionaires like Warren Buffet (Founder of Berkshire Hathaway), Jean and Steve Case (Founder of AOL) and

Joan and Richard Branson (Founder of Virgin Group) who have pledged to give most of their money away.

> *"Were we to use more than one percent of my claim checks [Berkshire Hathaway stock certificates] on ourselves, neither our happiness nor the well-being would be enhanced. In contrast, that remaining 99 percent can have a huge effect on the health and welfare of others."*
> —**Warren Buffett**

Other noted individuals have contributed or pledged large sums of their money to educational institutions, which serve the minds of those seeking knowledge.

One example is Jimmy Iovine, the previous CEO of Interscope Records, who teamed up with Rapper Dr. Dre to create Beats headphones, which they later sold to Apple. Jimmy is now a key Executive at Apple. He and Dr. Dre gave the University of Southern California (fight on!) over $70 million to create the USC Jimmy Iovine and Andre Young Academy for Arts, Technology and the Business of Innovation.

You can listen to Jimmy's 2009 USC commencement speech on YouTube. I was there to witness it and felt greatly inspired.

The Chan brothers, Partners of Hang Lung Group, gave $350 million to Harvard College. It was the second largest donation in history.

Robert Day, the Founder of a successful investment firm, gave $200 million to Claremont McKenna College.

The list is deep.

The money bequeathed to education alone could run several small countries.

But, what if you don't have that kind of money? Should you still shift to a life of service professionally?

—————◆—————

When I shifted from being a Media Technology Investment Banker to creating a firm to help people find their dream job, I ended up writing a book called *HIRED!* to help even more people. It felt great to match people with their true career passion.

I shifted even further toward helping companies engage and retain their employees. It's all about culture and making people feel valued.

I want people in any job to know that they do matter and that when they make a shift in their life in order to discover their true purpose, they find meaning and happiness.

———◆———

When I was told by a Pediatric Neurologist that one of my children was going to be half of his life behind, I was devastated. I was a Strategic Consultant for Fortune 100 corporations at the time and took some of my earnings to start an activity group for disabled toddlers. I called it *Mountain Climbers* and the local YMCA provided the teachers.

I later created a non-profit with three other parents of disabled children in order to raise money for special education classrooms throughout the county where I lived. The organization, *Dedication to Special Education*, is still thriving and I am so proud of what the new leaders have done to grow the non-profit.

I am not telling you this because I am anything special. I am telling you this because maybe Manoj has a point.

There are people like Bill and Lynne Twist, who founded and run Pachamama.org, which advocates for the indigenous tribes of the rainforest. Bill was in management consulting, equipment leasing, and financial services before shifting over to his purpose, which he says found him.

Many stay-at-home moms and dads leave jobs to raise their children, and many volunteer at their children's schools. I can tell you from experience (and you may know this already), that raising children is the toughest and most rewarding job in the world, and volunteering is sometimes like being back in corporate America. It takes just as much commitment and heart, just without the pay.

You have to truly have a calling to service to make these shifts, but, when you do, I agree with Manoj, it is fulfilling.

———◆———

Manoj is very comfortable with himself and his place in the world. He doesn't invest in material matters anymore. In fact, when I attended his lecture, he was in a t-shirt, a worn pair of weekend slacks and no shoes on his feet. I could tell he had found happiness and was free from suffering.

His expressions were relaxed and peaceful. I heard joy and excitement in his voice. And with certainty I knew that Manoj had found his purpose in teaching through engaging stories in order to inspire a path toward a life of happiness.

Manoj shifted from a society approved success seeker into a selfless man filled with compassion, empathy and love. He is exactly where he is supposed to be, without concern for where he is going.

I believe that Manoj is on his way to enlightenment. According to him, it is an ongoing path and no one should ever tell you that you are there. You are never really there, but you are always on the path.

He told me a great story about how Tom Brady opened up the door to his locker after winning SuperBowl XLIX, and there was a picture of Ginesha, the remover of obstacles, which he believes is his archetype.

Throughout his 2008 election, Obama is known to have carried a small Hanuman statuette in his pocket for inspiration. He still may. Hanuman represents leadership and service.

Howard Stern, the shock jock radio host, is said to have meditated every day for the past 25 years. This could attribute to how he became, arguably, one of the best interviewers in America because he listens and has peace within, regardless of his exterior persona.

Clint Eastwood and Jerry Seinfeld are also known to meditate via a practice called transcendental meditation where your personal guru gives you your own unique mantra.

———◆———

Manoj shared with me that my archetype is Lakshmi. Lakshmi embraces life with abundance both on a material and spiritual level. She is also the Goddess of Shri, that which gives luminosity and enables the creation of beauty in every aspect of our life.

"The lotus is like light. The lotuses in the two rear hands mean that you are emerging from the muck of life to be light and to shine with luminescence. The hand with the palm outside and reaching down represents blessings of material prosperity meaning you can enjoy a nice life, close relationships, and make a lot of money which will be an avenue of your helping others, but with an inner detachment to the actual money. The right hand with the palm out and fingers up comforts you and the fear of uncertainty is removed."

I have always felt these characteristics and was so encouraged to hear Manoj's confidence and assuredness that Lakshmi was my archetype. I am definitely going to get a statue of Lakshmi!

———◦———

Other wisdom shared by Manoj:

"If someone has a choice between a million dollars and enlightenment, they should choose the million dollars. The ego will be able to enjoy it more. With enlightenment, there is no ego to enjoy enlightenment; it is all heart."

"A doll made of salt is thrown into the ocean to measure the depth. It melts and loses itself. It loses its individuality, but it gains the infinite. It becomes enlightened."

"I have had many people come to my temple. I do not care from where they came. Sometimes I later learn that they are famous actors or directors or relatives of presidential politicians. It doesn't matter. We are all on our path and while our individual journeys may be different, we can all reach the place of bliss together."

———◦———

Manoj and his wife Jyothi's schedules are full to overflowing. They co-founded Unique Arts, a philosophy and speaking organization, and Vivekodayam, a non-profit Hindu deity temple, which means the rising of knowledge, resulting in a direct realization of who you are.

They mostly speak together now about Vedanta, yoga, Hindu deity archetypes, happiness, and enlightenment.

They talk to psychiatrists and psychologists, yoga teachers, and seekers of spiritual inspiration and guidance throughout the world. They speak at yoga festivals, yoga journal conferences, yoga studios, numerous organizations, ashrams, and universities.

When people are around Manoj and Jyothi, their faces light up. I can see hope in their eyes. The audience is growing. I can't wait to attend their next retreat.

Life is not permanent. We are always evolving. It's a fantastic journey.

Which Archetype Are You?

- GANESH
  - o Good fortune, prosperity, and success. The Lord of Beginnings and the Remover of Obstacles of both material and spiritual kinds.
  - o Ganesh will not only ground you, remove obstacles, and give you success, he leads you to self-knowledge. Anything new you would do such as a new job, new event, new teacher training, new day, etc., you get the blessings of Ganesh. He is the Lord of Thresholds.
- DANCING SHIVA (NATARAJA)
  - o One of three gods responsible for the creation, upkeep, and destruction of the world. The dance he performs is to destroy a tired universe and prepare it for a renewal by one of the other three gods.
  - o Nataraja is the archetype of anyone with radical change in their life, be it a new relationship, career, or a spiritual path. Shiva teaches us to embrace life with joy and a sense of wonder.
- DURGA
  - o Goddess who removes the negative energies that don't serve us both within as well as directed towards us.
- LAKSHMI
  - o Lakshmi teaches us to embrace life with abundance both material and spiritual. She is also the Goddess of Shri, that which gives

you luminosity and enables you to create beauty in every aspect of life.

- SARASWATI
  - o Goddess of knowledge, speech, intuitive wisdom, music, dance, and creativity.
- BUDDHA
  - o Buddha brings us calm, peace of mind, and ultimately spiritual awakening. In addition, the medicine Buddha from the Tibetan tradition heals you both in the body and mind.
- TARA
  - o Goddess of compassion, healing, and bringer of people to liberation.
- KRISHNA RADHA
  - o Krishna Radha is the archetype of the highest relationship where one sees the divine spirit as Shri Krishna in each other.

  HANUMAN
  - o Hanuman represents superhuman strength and superhuman intellect with a high degree of devotion. He resides in the heart chakra. If there is one deity who embodies Bhakti, it is Lord Hanuman.
- KALI
  - o Goddess Kali as an archetype completely transforms your life. She is goodness in a fierce form. She removes the negative energies that don't serve us. Ultimately, Ma Kali leads to enlightenment.
  - o Ma Kali kills the deepest ingrained patterns within and grants liberation.

Chapter 8 Takeaways

- When you find out what you are meant to do, you will become your authentic self.
- Trust the journey.
- The end result is to know yourself.
- Happiness comes from the inside. You will never satisfy the outside.
- You get the best movie of our life when you observe and you are not in it.
- The real obstacles in life are not external; they are within you.
- We are all connected.
- Self-actualization is the ultimate goal in life.
- Listen to other viewpoints. Stop fighting. Listen. Be humble.
- The core of life is joy. Seek joy.
- Once you know your archetype, meditate in front of your archetype and chant a mantra associated with your archetype. Then, open your eyes and look at your archetype figure. You will internalize into your subconscious and will awaken the archetype within you.
- There are many different waves in the ocean, just as there are many different traditions and paths. The commonality we all share is the ocean itself.
- You get the best movie of your life (and are the happiest) when you are not in the picture. This is one of the essential elements of Vedanta. Ask yourself: how are you when no one is looking?

PART FOUR

AFTER THE SHIFT

"Do not dwell in the past, do not dream of the future, concentrate the mind on the present moment."

— Buddha

Present

: *at this time; at hand*

: immediate

When we are young, we yearn for money, fame, things. We wonder— what will I do? How will I provide? Will I make it?

But, when we dig deeper and under the surface of our existence, what we discover is that what we really yearn for is to matter in this world.

We want to find meaning and to be engaged in our work. We want to live our days with joy and a sense of freedom.

We want to be happy.

When we don't feel that we matter or have a sense of personal happiness, then we feel alone.

We don't want to be alone.

What better feeling is there than to know that you are valued, that you are loved and that you are not alone?

———◦———

Between the lines and underneath the stories that you have read in *From Drift to Shift*, you will see that worth, love and happiness are at the core of everyone's shift, whether it be career or personal.

It doesn't matter if, on the outside, you are a CEO, a stay-at-home parent, an artist, or an entrepreneur. It is what is on the inside that unites us. It is our universal journey.

Sometimes it takes pain to drive us to what we are supposed to do and to who we are meant to be. Sometimes it's an internal pull or an external force. The point is; when we embrace the shift, we end up in a better place, regardless of any pain or apparent misfortune along the way.

And when we finally do get there, to the job we are meant to have, to the relationship that is our perfect match or to internal happiness that transcends any hardship; the focus turns to sustaining our new state of being.

———◦———

A study about happiness was conducted by Harvard psychiatrist, Robert Waldinger, and his team. They studied the lives of 724 men for over 75 years. Their main finding was that strong, close relationships are the foundation of happiness in life, whether in work or our personal life—it's not titles, money, or things.

When we have close relationships, even if it's only with one other person on the planet, we have the strength and feeling of support to maintain our shift. With that strength and sense of conviction comes happiness.

Sustaining that happiness on a lasting basis is what we all strive for.

———◦———

When you feel that your path is flowing, then there is a good chance that you should stay on it. Feeling good about where you are and where you are going is a key component to finding true meaning and happiness in work and in life.

When you feel good, more good comes your way. It is the natural flow of the universe. Don't block the good feelings. Don't block them in work or in your personal life. Don't just drift along in mediocrity. You are meant for great things in life. Embrace the shifts in your life. You are on the right path at all times, even if the path is not clear and perfect at all times.

If you focus on solutions rather than problems as you move forward, you will continue to move in a positive direction. Don't get mired in minutiae.

Look for the good. Good begets good, and when you are happy, it's all good.

NOW WHAT?

hen I was 18 and about to head off to college, I felt the need to attend a seminar or workshop before I left; something that would provide a major boost to my self-esteem. I had felt on my own since my parent's divorce several years earlier, but this time, I really would be.

I was about to put myself through college with every student loan that I could muster. I had no idea what I wanted to do in life or how I would pay back the money. I was scared to go out on my own and needed something to sustain me through this new chapter that was 100 percent on and about me.

After a great deal of research, I chose a self-awareness program near my home in San Diego. It proved to be a weekend of awakening.

One of the rules of the workshop was that we had to be completely honest in all that we said and did. For example, there was an activity where we had to stand in total silence in front of the person we were most attracted to in the room. I came close to picking my second choice. At the last minute I thought *what the hell.* After all, I was in a contained and safe environment and was constantly encouraged to allow vulnerability in. So, I turned left instead of right and stood in front of my number one. It just so happened that he was attracted to me, too. Pretty intense. I could have easily been rejected, which is so often the case in life. But, this time…well, it sure pumped me up.

I looked around and saw that there were at least 20 people standing around me and even more around him. It was a heady moment that I will never forget. I felt loved and special. When we feel this in our relationships and in work, there is no limit to what we can achieve.

According to research performed at the University of Warwick, results from a study in the economics department revealed that when people are happy, they work 12 percent harder. If we love what we do and doing what we love, it should not feel like work. If we are in a relationship we love and are loved in that relationship, it should not feel like work.

The key, from my perspective, is to feel happy. When we feel happy, we become even more happy. Good things come our way. For me, at the age of 18, I needed some happy to help me move forward with confidence.

Another assignment during the weekend workshop was to go into nature and bring back something that said, *this is me*. I love being outside. Marshmallow clouds, the powerful force of the ocean, birds of all types squawking overhead, a salamander bobbing its head…nature is all of God's creations wrapped in a chaotic, beautiful bow.

My ego wanted me to pick a seashell to represent how I would ride the waves to distant, exciting shores; or to choose something like a feather to show that I had the strength to let go and trust the wind to guide me. It all sounded poetic, but I knew what I was.

I was a weed.

I grew everywhere and nowhere and, once in

**Mustard seed weed on
California hillside**

a while, in between. On that particular weekend, I happened to be everywhere. I plucked the first one of me that I came across. It was a big one with sticky green, hairy stalks shooting in all directions.

Aside from its permeation, what I have always loved most about the mustard weed are the little clumps of brilliant yellow at the end of each random arm. In the spring, if you look into the hills throughout California, it's as though the sun itself has swathed a path of brightness along the green, creating a road to somewhere you want to go.

I hid the mustard weed under my shirt and when it was my turn to speak before the group of 100 or so, as nervous as I was, I held my weed up high and said, "I am light." I believed it, too.

Decades later, I attended a workshop at a mountain yoga studio.

I read the guest speaker's bio on the brochure. It talked about shifts in life, Hindu deities, and embracing happiness. I knew I was in the right place.

When Manoj stood in front of the eager audience, he asked each of us our name.

"Jody, your name means light."

Thank you Manoj.

Sometimes it is hard to see where your path is going or to know if you are even on it, especially if it involves tragedy, health issues, or a sense of despair; but if you pay attention to how you feel and the signs that appear (such as someone coming into your life and affirming an inkling you may have), it will become clear.

When I risked standing in front of the person I was most attracted to at the weekend seminar and when I raised the mustard weed for all to see, I felt excited and alive. I felt good. Somewhere inside I knew I was on a path to somewhere good, even if I didn't yet know where. It didn't matter. I had faith in me and the anxiety about the unknown subsided.

Sometimes, we block our path. We let circumstances, people, or negative thoughts prevent us from continuing on the road to happiness and fulfillment in work or in life.

The challenge lies in releasing the negative and focusing on the positive so that our path can open up for us. When it is open, we are inspired, driven, excited, and joyful. When it is closed, we are filled with self-doubt, jealousy, depression, or external blame.

———◆———

Even if things are going well when we make a major shift in our life, we can sabotage our experience by questioning our success and happiness.

We feel guilty for feeling good.

Do you ever tell yourself that you shouldn't enjoy your independence, your happiness, or your feeling of freedom even though you are doing what you love and have relationships that bring you joy?

Shifts can be wonderful things, but at times are so fresh and new that we need time to adjust.

When you buy a new house in an area you have always dreamed of living, and perhaps you have stretched a bit financially to get there, you may experience buyer's remorse.

Guilt. Fear. Uncertainty.

After a while, when you have moved your things in, settled into your morning cup of coffee, and snuggled into your new cloud comforter, you begin to adapt. Maybe you sleep in a few extra minutes because you haven't slept in in years, or you take the time to enjoy the view you now have.

Give yourself time. Time to settle into your new post-shift reality.

When I was in Paris doing research for an upcoming novel, I sat in Le Coup Chou, the restaurant that journalists Kati Morton and Richard Holbrooke used to frequent on the Left Bank, and read Morton's memoire. I took the time to linger over a spinach salad and a glass of wine in the middle of the afternoon while surrounded by 14th-century stone walls and worn tables.

I loved it, but I felt guilty. Why? Because I wasn't being productive as we are so often taught in our fast paced lives. I was simply enjoying the food, the book, the moment—and felt guilty for it.

And then something happened.

As I sat there, I decided to brush my guilt aside for just a few moments and wonder who else might have eaten in this very old social gathering place. What did they wear? I pictured them in layers of velvet and linen that were too hot for a humid Paris afternoon. How did they eat? Did they use forks and knives or just rip the meat off a turkey leg with their teeth? I became so curious that I let my mind wander and imagine people from hundreds of years ago sitting across the table from me. I heard how they spoke just by letting go and letting my imagination take over. Writers do that a lot.

I felt invigorated. Invigorated because I was thoroughly enjoying my lazy afternoon in a magical place on a tiny side street in the middle of Paris. I had a new appreciation of the world and me in it.

Deep in my being I knew that a major shift was coming. Being in Paris with just me to keep me company, led me to eventually appreciate *me*. I needed this time to understand that I was ready for something grand.

What came later was the idea for a novel, a lot of outlining and character development, further traipsing across Paris for scene details and, ultimately, an offer to read it from four agents at a writing conference I later attended.

Let go of guilt. Trust. Be inspired. Shift.

Traveling to the Amazon to visit the Achuar tribe deep in the rainforest was a big one. While I wanted to understand their simple, yet fulfilling way of life, to experience their dream culture ceremonies, and to see what it was like to not wear makeup for nine days; what I really wanted was to understand myself.

It wasn't until after the shift that I learned to accept the actions I had taken in my personal life and to feel that I could stand strong, as a newly single woman. I could sustain my new existence regardless of what life threw my way.

Even if I was unsure of how I would get there, I gained confidence that I was on a path to a more fulfilling career and life based on my deepest passions and dreams. I had shifted and now the journey would be a brand new one that no longer gave me pause. No need to worry. I was ready.

After visiting with Manoj at the yoga retreat, I felt that a new kind of happiness was on my horizon.

I could leave the guilt of exiting my marriage, for keeping my emotions bottled up, and for not being true to myself on the doorstep, and let in a different type of joy.

It takes time and every day is not perfect. When you make a shift, give yourself time. It's all about the flow of life.

Relax. Breathe. Time is on your side.

I think another way to deal with shifting is to reach out and reach back for support as you travel on your new path. Maybe it's that friend you hung out with as a kid and lost touch with or the teacher who had an impact on you. It could be the neighbor down the street who brought you soup when you were sick or the business mentor who always encouraged you.

Reach out and reconnect. There is something about coming full circle with your positive past that helps you adjust to your new, exciting, and sometimes uncertain world.

Recently, a good friend who I had been in touch with after a 25-year lapse came to town for a visit. Time rewound instantly and then I lost track of it. We sat in the lounge area of one of San Francisco's landmark hotels for nine hours. I laughed, cried, we exchanged stories, memories, and opinions, and had a lovely day.

I felt nothing but comfort, contentment, a sense of grounding, and a place in the world. I have known this friend since the age of 5. We lived a block apart.

I went to my first concert in New York City with him and a pack of other 13 year olds. I was a cheerleader for our high school's winning football team that he played on. In a way, he is like a brother or a close cousin, and I know that for the rest of my life, he will be there for me.

In Eddie Vedder's song "Just Breathe," the one that helped Andy stay alive by reminding him to breathe, there is another part of the song that has always spoken to me:

> *I'm a lucky man*
> *To count on two hands*
> *The ones I love.*

> *Some folks just have one.*
> *Others, they have none.*
> *Uh huh.*

Whenever I hear those lyrics, I find myself literally counting my closest friends and confidantes on my fingers. I say their names out loud as I go and smile because I do fill two hands.

Try it. Count the ones you love. If you have even one, you are lucky. If you don't have any, you are wrong. Go back in time. Open your heart. Count.

Then, reach out to them even if you haven't for many years. Contact that person who matters to you, even if they don't know that they do. There is something so complete in connecting with others that know you and have known you and love you exactly as you are. They are your true support system in life and, when you go through any shift—good, bad, radical—you already know who will be there for you. Hold them close and let the others go.

Once you have connected, stay in touch. Connecting feeds our soul. A phone call, a text, an email, a handwritten note.

I wanted to share my friend's thank you note, the old fashioned handwritten note that I received in the mail. I will save it with my other special keepsakes.

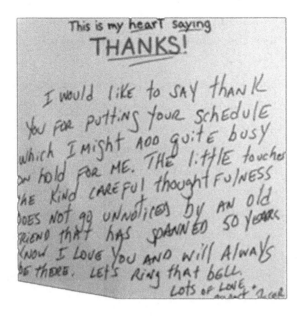

This is my heart saying
THANKS!

I would like to say thank you for putting your schedule which I might add quite busy on hold for ME. THE little touches the kind careful thoughtfulness does not go unnoticed by an old friend that has spanned 50 years now I love You and will always be there. let's ring that bell. Lots of love

Once you shift, you also have to let go.

- Let go of self-loathing.
- Let go of judging.
- Let go of pushing or trying to control.
- Let go of absorbing others' emotions.
- Let go of not being your true self.
- Let go.

Sloan was my roommate in the Pi Beta Phi Sorority in college. I recently learned that she and I applied to The University of California at Santa Barbara and agreed to go without ever having seen the school. We both did it completely on our own. No one helped us.

I admired Sloan throughout college. To me, Sloan was perfect and I was not. She was beautiful, patient, kind, soft spoken, the perfect weight (I was fluffy) and seemed to be God's chosen.

We lost touch for many years because I was off trying to figure out life in places like New York City, which was across the country from where we had spent time together.

But as the internet grew and Facebook evolved, I found Sloan again. We met up at a sorority reunion and spent many hours talking. I admitted to her on one of our walks that I never felt good enough. She told me how I had helped her mend her broken heart and that she loved me so.

What was I thinking for all of those years? We are all good enough, just as we are at every point along the way.

Many of us are so hard on ourselves as we try to navigate this journey called life. Isn't it better and a more natural path of least resistance to accept ourselves or, heaven forbid, love ourselves?

There is no perfect person on the planet and we are not as bad as we think we are.

I believe that one of the joys of life is that we are meant to connect in a meaningful, loving, non-judgmental way with ourselves and with others.

When we do, we find meaning and purpose in our work and our life. Why? Because we are happy.

I met Brad Feld decades ago and I had no idea if he remembered me, but I did know that I wanted to ask him to write the Foreword to *From Drift to Shift*. Not only did he deliver with heart and openness, he introduced me to Jerry, who is an amazing person and incredible leader. At first, when reading about Jerry's background, you may have thought that he might be unapproachable. To be a key player of JP Morgan's venture arm is pretty impressive. If you were a company or investment banker, you would be lucky to get a moment of his time as he was in mega demand.

Jerry values time so much now and he takes the time to really engage in life. He listens, he lets vulnerability guide him, and he is a champion for others. Jerry is one of the most approachable people I have met and am so appreciative for his honesty and perspective. If you are a start-up company and have the chance to attend one of his weekend boot camps, I highly recommend it. But, brace yourself. You will find out who you really are and I bet you will come out a better leader because of it.

———◆———

I knew Darren before his accident and know him even better now. The courage he has shown in life is beyond comprehension. His will to move forward, try new things, share his talent, and connect is catching. When you are with Darren, it's all about love and time. Time is all we have and Darren uses his to inspire and paint and show the world that he cares.

———◆———

I met Andy through mutual friends. When we sat down to talk about his story, I was nervous. We met at a cool café in Tahoe and he bought me coffee—a gentleman from the start. It took about one minute for me to relax because Andy is so filled with compassion, empathy, concern for the environment, passion for helping vets, and the disabled. His list of appreciation is endless and he brings forth high energy for each and every purpose. He loves his work running Squaw and Alpine and he loves spending time with others. He is a great listener and offers to help at every turn. There aren't enough pages to tell you all of the incredible things Andy has done for others, and how, despite almost losing his own life, he is inspired to continue to give back.

———◆———

Serita and Reid are smart, funny and self-effacing. They have found a way to rise above the cards they were dealt when they came into the world. I just want to be around them. Their enthusiasm for the growth of iFoster is contagious. I can't wait to be a part of their holiday gift program and to accompany them to one of their job boot camps for foster kids whom they place in promising careers. I went to a party at their house where each room had a theme. It was one of the most fun nights for me. I love their spontaneity, commitment, and passion for their work and for each other.

———◆———

I met Emilee when I took a Pilates class from her for the first time. I had no idea what Pilates was, but I wanted to strengthen my flimsy core and was told by several people that Emilee was the girl to see. I sat outside her private studio room as she finished up with an over 80-year-old woman ahead of me. (Who looks 60!) When the session was over, Emilee gave the woman a big hug and offered encouraging words. I could tell they were not just instructor/client, they were friends. I knew I was in the right place.

When Emilee shared her story of shifting through cancer, I knew that life was too short to focus on anything but happiness. Emilee lives and loves in the moment and has become a close friend.

As I reflect on the writing of *From Drift to Shift*, I notice another theme that has come out of the writing of this book.

Time.

How do you use your time?

Do you use it to support you, your dreams, your goals, your relationships? Or do you use it to knock yourself down, judge others, and blame?

When it comes to work, do you find that when you are not engaged with your true purpose or passion, that you waste time? Or do you find that you use every minute to your advantage because you are so excited at moving your work forward?

Here's how, like the people in this book, you know that you have become the person you are meant to be: Time (or lack of it) is no longer of concern. You are in the zone. Time holds no meaning for you anymore because you are happy.

Look for the signs.

When I set out to write *From Drift to Shift*, I paid very close attention to the people that crossed my path, the articles and books I read, the conversations around me, and the randomness of my experiences.

I looked for signs that I was on the right path with the book, the choice of the inspiring people to include, and the message I wanted to convey.

I saw signs everywhere, which gave me added confidence that I was moving in the right direction. Some of the signs included:

- The word 'shift' appeared in almost every article I read.
- People talked to me about how their life was drifting or shifting without knowing the title of my book.
- When I discussed the essence of *From Drift to Shift* with people, every single one asked when it would be available because they were going to get a copy for themselves *and* a friend.
- My followers on Twitter and on my website grew.
- The writing flowed effortlessly.
- The right Editor showed up.
- The right Publicist showed up.
- The cover matched the message.
- Everyone got their story comments back to me and they were minimal.
- I was ahead of my publishing deadline.

When I felt confirmed by the signs, I was able to move the project forward with almost no effort. If I felt resistance at any turn, I knew the path needed to shift.

When you see the signs that point you in the direction you should go with your work and life, you will then get impulses and ideas and you will take action. The whole process will seem natural and effortless. It will all fall into place for you. Pay attention to the signs in your life.

You may have heard of the *six degrees of separation*; that at some point we are all related.

Well, in From *Drift to Shift*, I find the overlap quite fascinating. Eight people whose lives cross and converge and share many of the same challenges. These are people who have never met one another. I am their only link. As I interviewed people whose stories I wanted to have in the book, I knew that I wanted a diversity of backgrounds, careers, relationships, and challenges. And, most importantly, I wanted to include amazing people that the reader would relate to as their own life experienced shifts along the way.

I didn't realize at the time how much similarity there would be between them.

Life Experience Overlaps

- Struggled with parents/family
- Experienced depression
- Experienced life-threatening challenges
- Are high achievers
- Sought spiritual direction
- Experienced childhood trauma
- Changed careers more than twice

In a way, we are all related and that's a beautiful thing. I believe that we can rely on one another along our paths, even if we are not in the same profession or stage of life. There is always someone with similar experiences.

———◆———

You are meant to be truly happy in your work and in your life. This is your destiny.

In order to do this, you must follow your true nature, your inner bliss, the career and the relationships that make you happy.

Living a life more fully than you ever have before—this is what we all seek. And yes, we all have so much in common; we have each other. That's a beautiful thing.

Self Portrait

It doesn't interest me if there is one God
or many gods.
I want to know if you belong or feel
abandoned.
If you know despair or can see it in others.
I want to know
if you are prepared to live in the world
with its harsh need
to change you. If you can look back
with firm eyes
saying this is where I stand. I want to know
if you know
how to melt into that fierce heat of living
falling toward
the center of your longing. I want to know
if you are willing
to live, day by day, with the consequence of love
and the bitter
unwanted passion of your sure defeat.
I have heard, in *that* fierce embrace, even
the gods speak of God.
—**David Whyte** from *Fire in the Earth*

Now What Takeaways

- Stay curious. Show sincere interest in others. You will learn much.
- Don't settle in life. Go after your dream. Go get it.
- If you let fear, money, or power drive you, happiness will not be yours.
- If you let your heart guide you, happiness will always be yours.
- Read. Keep a notebook of advice and perspectives that resonate with you. Refer to it often.
- Be an encourager, not a naysayer.
- Help others whenever you can. Karma is real.
- Reach out to old friends and reconnect. You will discover that love is all around you.
- Surround yourself with people that support you. Let go of those who don't.
- Ask questions.
- Risk, even if you are afraid.
- Listen. Learn. Repeat.
- Focus on the good, in yourself and in others. More good will come your way and your life will be full.
- Don't beat yourself up if you're not where you think you should be. The journey is the key to happiness. Be happy in the moment. Be happy with now.

- You are doing great. You are on your way to even greater.
- Allow yourself to be happy. Let go of guilt.
- Go with the flow of life. Don't try to control it all; you'll miss the joy of the journey.
- When you shift and land in the job, relationship, life of your dreams, keep on living. Life has so much to offer.
- Seek to feel good. Feelings lead your thoughts and thoughts become things. Feel good, think good thoughts, and watch good things happen in your work and in your life.
- Look for the signs that it is time to shift. The signs are there. It is your job to notice them and then act as they show you the way.
- Trust your instincts.
- Inspiration is your greatest gauge as to whether you are moving forward on your path.
- Be true to yourself at all times.
- You are unique. You matter.
- Your contribution to this world is a great thing that others will value.
- Have fun. Relax. Embrace where you are and where you are going. It's all good!
- Think happy thoughts. Start with the easy ones. Keep after it until you feel happy. When you feel happy, great things happen.
- Seek clarity. Stay present. Listen intently. Communicate clearly. Be positive. Appreciate those around you.
- Love yourself first and foremost.
- Be an outlier. Be outside the norm. You are above the average. Be exceptional. Trust your instincts. Be the real you. You matter.
- When you have found happiness, you have achieved success.

APPENDIX

iFOSTER JOBS PROGRAM

iFOSTER LAPTOP PROGRAM

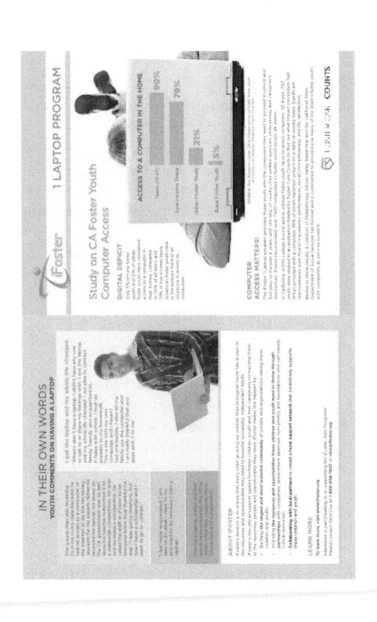

iFOSTER HOUSE OF REPRESENTATIVES BILL

....

(Original Signature of Member)

114TH CONGRESS

2D SESSION $\text{H. R. }11$

To amend the Internal Revenue Code of 1986 to include foster care transition youth as members of targeted groups for purposes of the work opportunity credit.

IN THE HOUSE OF REPRESENTATIVES

Mr. MCDERMOTT introduced the following bill; which was referred to the Committee on llllllllllllll

A BILL

To amend the Internal Revenue Code of 1986 to include foster care transition youth as members of targeted groups for purposes of the work opportunity credit.

1 Be it enacted by the Senate and House of Representatives

2 of the United States of America in Congress assembled,

3 SECTION 1. SHORT TITLE.

4 This Act may be cited as the "Improved Employment

5 Outcomes for Foster Youth Act of 2016".

6201 C:\USERS\FLHECK~1\APPDATA\ROAMING\SOFTQUAD\

XMETAL\7.0\GEN\C\MCDERM~1.X

July 13, 2016 (5:49 p.m.)

F:\M14\MCDERM\MCDERM_059.XML

f:\VHLC\071316\071316.292.xml (635365|14)

2

1 SEC. 2. INCLUSION OF FOSTER CARE TRANSITION YOUTH

2 FOR PURPOSES OF WORK OPPORTUNITY

3 CREDIT.

4 (a) IN GENERAL. —Section 51(d)(1) of the Internal

5 Revenue Code of 1986 is amended by striking "or" at the

6 end of subparagraph (I), by striking the period at the end

7 of subparagraph (J) and inserting ", or", and by adding

8 at the end the following new subparagraph:

9 "(K) a qualified foster care transition

10 youth.".

11 (b) QUALIFIED FOSTER CARE TRANSITION YOUTH

12 DEFINED. —Section 51(d) of such Code is amended by

13 adding at the end the following new paragraph:

14 "(16) QUALIFIED FOSTER CARE TRANSITION

15 YOUTH. —The term 'qualified foster care transition

16 youth' means any individual who is certified by the

17 designated local agency as—

18 "(A) not having attained age 27 as of the

19 hiring date, and

20 "(B) having been in foster care (within the

21 meaning of section 477 of the Social Security

22 Act), after attaining the younger of—

23 "(i) age 16, and

24 "(ii) the age specified in subsection

25 (a)(7) of such section.".

6201 C:\USERS\FLHECK~1\APPDATA\ROAMING\SOFTQUAD\

XMETAL\7.0\GEN\C\MCDERM~1.X

July 13, 2016 (5:49 p.m.)

F:\M14\MCDERM\MCDERM_059.XML

f:\VHLC\071316\071316.292.xml (635365|14)

3

1 (c) EFFECTIVE DATE. —The amendments made by

2 this section shall apply with respect to individuals who

3 begin work for the employer after the date of the enact4-

ment of this Act.

01 C:\USERS\FLHECK~1\APPDATA\ROAMING\SOFTQUAD\
XMETAL\7.0\GEN\C\MCDERM~1.X
July 13, 2016 (5:49 p.m.)
F:\M14\MCDERM\MCDERM_059.XML
f:\VHLC\071316\071316.292.xml (635365|14)

The Mission Of The Pachamama Alliance

To empower indigenous people of the Amazon rainforest to preserve their lands and culture and, using insights gained from that work, to educate and inspire individuals everywhere to bring forth a thriving, just, and sustainable world.

Vision

The vision that informs the Pachamama Alliance's work is of a world that works for everyone: an environmentally sustainable, spiritually fulfilling, socially just human presence on this planet—a New Dream for humanity.

Purpose

The Pachamama Alliance's unique contribution is to generate and engage people everywhere in transformational conversations and experiences consistent with this purpose. It weaves together indigenous and modern worldviews such that human beings are in touch with their dignity and are ennobled by the magnificence, mystery, and opportunity of what is possible for humanity at this time.

It is here to inspire and galvanize the human family to generate a critical mass of conscious commitment to a thriving, just, and sustainable way of life on Earth. This is a commitment to transforming human systems and structures that separate us, and to transforming our relationships with ourselves, with one another, and with the natural world.

Underlying Assumptions

- If present trends continue, the probable future for life on Earth will be defined by periods of substantial social, environmental, and economic disruption, if not complete collapse.

- Humanity already possesses sufficient resources, technology, and know-how to reverse these trends. What is missing is the sense of urgency and the popular and political will to act.
- Without concentrated human intervention, certain tipping points will be reached that will make our present trajectory irreversible.

Guiding Values and Principles

- The universe is friendly and the evolutionary force that put the stars in motion is still moving through all of us and is a dynamic, self-organizing process whose grace and guidance we can trust.
- Human beings are by nature collaborative and cooperative and innately desire the success of the human species and all life. When barriers to our natural expression are eliminated (i.e. resignation, myths of separation, and scarcity), we cooperate for the common, long-term good.
- Human beings are not separate from each other or nature. We are totally interrelated and our actions have consequences to all. What we do to others we do to ourselves. What we do to Earth we do to ourselves.
- Indigenous people are the source of a worldview and cosmology that can provide powerful guidance and teachings for achieving our vision—a thriving, just, and sustainable world.
- One of the most effective ways to produce results is to empower other organizations through skillful alliances. Amazing things can be accomplished when people stop worrying about who gets the credit.
- People's actions are correlated with how they see the world—the story they tell themselves about the world. Transforming the way that people see and relate to the world and the possibilities they see for the future is a powerful way to effect social change.
- Consciously and unconsciously created systems of ongoing oppression and inequality exist in the world. The outcomes generated by those systems are directly in opposition to our vision of a thriving, just, and sustainable world.

We are accountable to—and stand in solidarity with—those whose access to material resources and free self-expression is limited by unjust systems of power and privilege.

August 9th is International Day of the World's Indigenous Peoples. It was proclaimed by the United Nations in an effort to protect and promote the rights of the indigenous populations of the world. Be sure to celebrate the indigenous peoples and their practices!

www.pachamama.org

A Detailed Explanation
Of The Hindu Deities

Yogic Deities as Archetypes

Often when you visit a yoga studio or an ashram or just about anywhere in India, you see Hindu and Buddhist deities such as Ganesh, Shiva, Lakshmi, etc. You can understand and approach a deity at many levels. The easiest way to relate to them is as your personal archetype.

What is an Archetype?

The word 'archetype' was coined by the Swiss psychotherapist Carl Jung. An archetype is a symbol or a form that is imprinted in your subconscious. Jung was inspired by the yogic archetypes and originally called them devis and devas or Shiva and Shakti. Later on, he amended them to anima (feminine) and animus (masculine) archetypes.

You may have archetypes from many traditions. For instance, the Sun god is called Ra (Amun Ra) in the Egyptian tradition. The same Sun god in the Roman tradition is called Mitra while in the yogic/hindu tradition, the Sun god is also Mitra or Surya. Even though the cultures were thousands of miles and thousands of years apart, these are universal archetypes. Interestingly, Mitra was born of a virgin mother on December 25th, was a wandering preacher with 12 disciples, and was resurrected three days after he died. The cross is another beautiful archetypical symbol. The Hawaiians identify these archetypes as Aumakua like Pele, goddess of the fire and volcano. There are many archetypes from Greek traditions such as Athena, Isis, Zeus, etc. however these yogic archetypes such as Ganesh, Shiva, Lakshmi, Durga, etc. have persisted for more time and with a larger following. The entire philosophy of yogic self-realization is embedded in the symbols of these archetypes.

These archetypes are within our collective unconscious. These archetypes lie deeply embedded in our causal body and are available for the whole human race. They pop up in times of transition in our lives and help guide us to achieve higher ideals. One of the biggest realizations about ourselves is to know who our archetype is and how to invoke that and incorporate those superhuman ideals in our lives. At its very core, these teachings are not a religion (theism, polytheism, monotheism, etc.) nor a philosophy (dualism, monism, non-dualism, etc.). It is a Sadhana (spiritual practice) of actualizing human potential of becoming the best at every stage of our lives. It is always perfecting as opposed to perfection and looking at the good in everything around us.

The Sanskrit word for archetype is Ishtadevata. Ishta means desired and devata means deity. I feel Ishtadevata is more heart oriented than the intellectual sounding archetype.

These murtis (statues) exist within you as archetypes. They are there to help you through transformation and lead you to awakening. As Joseph Campbell said, "Myths are collective dreams while your dreams are personal myths! When your personal dreams, hopes, and aspirations are in tune with the collective myths, there is amazing harmony in your life."

How to Find Your Archetype (Ishtadevata)

It is like falling in love: the form of the deity has to appeal to you. It is like walking into a room of new people and liking someone off the bat or going into an art museum and connecting with a piece of art.

Similarly, I encourage you to look at these deities, touch them, feel them, understand their symbolisms and myths. Sooner than later, you will find yourself gravitating to one, two, or three deities. Usually you have one primary archetype and several secondary ones. They change during your life because you change.

These archetypes give you the reason to live with joy and help you in your personal, professional, and spiritual aspects of your life. They also remind us of the grander ideals we can all live for. They bring out the yearning some of us have to make an impact on people and society and leave a legacy beyond the transitory nature of our lives.

Murtis or Yogic Statues

When the yogic statues are energized, they are often termed as murtis. A murti can be made of metal (brass or bronze), stone, or marble and is usually on the main altars (sanctum sanctorum) in temples. You can energize these murtis in a couple of ways. One technique is called Prana Pratishta where a priest invokes Vedic mantras to imbibe prana into the murti. This is usually done in temples. I don't recommend this method for most householders because you then have to do puja every day to the murti and dress and feed the murti. We live busy lives and it's difficult to meet this commitment. What I recommend is Mantra Pratishta where the murtis are energized by mantras. You can actually measure the energy in these murtis by a technique called GDV (Gas Discharge Visualization), which is an enhancement of the aura photography technique (Kirlian effect). Several companies had made these measurements on murtis and have shown they hold energy and that's why the murtis need to be metal, stone, or marble.

Are These Archetypes Part of the Hindu Religion?

Firstly, Hinduism is not a religion, a fact is not known to most people. Hinduism is a set of spiritual practices to realize the self. This is called Sanatana Dharma, the dharmic living to realize the eternal self. It has never been a religion. When the British came to India several centuries ago, they found the Indians engaged in various spiritual practices such as asana, meditation, chanting, tantric rituals, etc. The Western mind, which was used to a monotheistic religion was quite frankly mystified and tried to make sense of the whole thing. At that time, the people of the Indus Valley river civilization were called Hindus by the Persian traders. So, the British came up with the name Hinduism and coined it as a religion. The Hindu tradition has always been based on spiritual practices to realize the self.

At first sight, these deities may appear as polytheistic. When you go deeper, you realize that they are different facets of the When you go deeper into the teachings of the Upanishads (Advaita Vedanta), you realize that it's actually non-dualism. You cannot objectify the self, it is the eternal 'I Am.' If you talk or even think about it, it's not that. That's why it's termed non-dualism or Advaita (not two).

The origin of these deities comes from the Puranic scriptures, which is often called the fifth Veda. Often the Vedic philosophy of the Upanishads is extremely rigorous, complex, and requires years of study under a guru who is a Shrotriya Brahmanishta (one who is enlightened and can teach you the method in the Upanishads). Most people in ancient India had regular jobs and businesses and didn't have the time to commit to such a study, not unlike modern day. That's why these deities with their myths and symbols came about to explain the same philosophies in very vivid and colorful detail. Most children in India grow up with these myths. Storytelling is an important art in this tradition.

Working with Your Archetype

Create an altar and meditate in front of your deity. You may set up an altar anywhere in your home and make it a sacred space for you to have a daily meditation practice. Place your deity archetype on a cloth and decorate the altar with candles, flowers, incense, pictures of teachers, or anyone meaningful in your life. You may have multiple archetypes however you meditate only on one deity at a time because the energies are different. The time spent in meditation is totally up to you. It's more important to be natural and relaxed while meditating and not try to still the mind. Instead of trying to quench the thoughts (which takes a lifetime of practice, if not more, and is the entire premise of Patanjali yoga), you focus on the gap or the space between your thoughts. This gap is pure consciousness because your thoughts are overlaid on consciousness. This gap is similar to the gap between mantras so mantra-based meditation may be useful here. When thoughts recede, your mind is suffused with pure consciousness. In this state, your mind is like a vacuum. You then open your eyes to the deity in front of you. Subconsciously, your mind starts sucking in the deity's attributes and qualities and you slowly start to awaken the archetype within you. This is a simple but powerful technique that yogis have been doing over the years.

Four Practices You Can Do with Your Archetype

When you want to work with your archetype towards spiritual awakening, elevate your archetype to pure consciousness. Pure consciousness is without form and beyond time and space. However, our minds come from time and space and cannot fathom the unfathomable. Here is where these archetypes come in.

There are four practices to incorporate the murti (statue) of your archetype in your life. One practice is meditation and the other three are in your daily life because yoga is everywhere and not just to be performed inside a room. These practices are adapted from the teachings of the Bhagavad Gita.

1) Karma Yoga: View any event in your life as a prasad (gift) from your archetype. It's like when you visit a temple, a priest sanctifies some almonds in front of the deity and gives it to you as prasad. You accept it gratefully and don't demand for ice cream! Similarly, you view any event in your life, be it good or bad, as a prasad from your Ishtadevata. This weakens the feelings of doer-ship by the ego. This is the single most important sadhana we can do in today's society. This deceptively simple but consistent practice brings great peace of mind.

2) Meditation: Do this in front of your archetype and open your eyes to its essence. This brings out the "devatabhava" (feeling of godliness) within you. This is Raja yoga and is the eight-fold path of yogic path of Lord Patanjali.

3) Puja and Bhakti Yoga: This practice opens your heart chakra. This feeling of love to the divine affects the feelings/emotions part of the mind. Kirtan chanting to your deity is an important aspect of this practice.

4) Jnana Yoga: Understand the philosophy, symbolisms, and mythology. This affects the intellect part of your mind. We are literally reliving all the myths of the gods and goddesses.

Our mind has four components and each type of yoga addresses a different component:

- Ego is the subtlest aspect of the mind. Karma yoga deals with this sense of doer-ship.
- Buddhi is the intellect part of the mind. Jnana yoga helps to understand the symbolisms of your archetype and their myths.

- Chittha is the unconsciousness part of the mind where impressions are stored. Meditation in front of your archetype and the eight-fold path of Raja yoga of Lord Patanjali deals with this.
- Manas is the feelings/emotions part of your mind. Bhakti yoga is the path that refines this aspect of the mind.

The easiest way to understand the four aspects of the mind is to do a thought experiment: Suppose there is a fire in the room you are in. The sense organs detect the fire and relay it to the Manas part of the mind. The intellect, Buddhi, then consults with the Chittha and determines that somewhere in the past you have been burnt and fire is not good. The Buddhi then tells the five organs of action (Karma Indriyas) to get out of the room (hopefully the room has multiple exits). What does the ego do? It actually does nothing; it rushes in to claim ownership that I did this!

You work on all these four aspects of the mind by doing these types of yoga together. Ultimately, you start cutting the strands this dualistic world has on you. Finally, the last strand is cut not by you (or your ego) but by grace. This is a direct and intuitive realization that you are the self and not the body or mind. It is an identity shift as opposed to an experience of samadhi and characterized by a state where one is practicing samadhi all the time. This is awakening.

The Deities: By Dr. Manoj Chalam of Unique Arts

GANESH (Ganesha)

Mantra: Om Gam Ganapataye Namah

Summary: Ganesh not only grounds you, but also removes obstacles and brings you success. He leads you to self-knowledge. Anything new you would do such as a new job, new event, new training, new day, etc., you get the blessings of Ganesh. He is the Lord of Thresholds.

Ganesh is considered to be the remover of obstacles, bringing protection to you and your family. Ultimately, he leads you to enlightenment. As you know,

Ganesh removes obstacles in a physical sense with the weapons he holds in either hand. However, the real way he removes obstacles in our lives is with a mouse at his feet. (If the Ganesh murti doesn't come with a mouse, then your mind is the mouse and you make Ganesha complete!). The mouse is the transport vehicle (Vahana) of Ganesh. In other words, he rides on the mouse. However, the mouse symbolizes our minds which wander all over the place like the way the mouse scampers around. By riding on the mouse, Ganesh controls the mouse, therefore controlling and stilling our minds. Ganesh thus gets you in a state called Practicing Samadhi where the thought patterns in your mind are uniform. In that state, you do not experience any obstacle. So the obstacles we face in our lives are not outside you but inside our mind as vrittis (thought fluctuations). Ganesh removes obstacles by giving you an inner calmness.

Surrender to Ganesh. The abhaya mudra (blessing gesture with his hand) is very powerful. It means, when you surrender your ego and yourself to Ganesh, he will dispel all fears and insecurities from within you. Just do your duty (Karma yoga) and leave all the results to Ganesh. We have far less control over our lives than what we think.

The trunk of Ganesh symbolizes the ability of discernment (Viveka). Just like the way an elephant can carry a heavy log with his trunk or pick a single blade of grass with the same trunk, we need to have the ability to discern in our dealings with people. The ultimate discernment is seeing the unity of consciousness in this world of multiplicity. The twisted trunk of Ganesha is called vakratunda. This represents the path of sadhana, spiritual practice. An elephants trunk usually hangs down, this is the path of least resistance in the New Age, which says you are already enlightened and don't need to do any work. The twisted trunk of Ganesha represents that the path of Sadhana that leads to the sweet he holds, the bliss of enlightenment, satcitananda. Sat is truth of what Is, the 'I Am.' Chit is Awareness. Ananda is bliss. So when you are truly aware of the self, the 'I Am,' the only thing there is, you are in bliss. This is the sweetness Ganesha wants us to taste.

The broken tusk of Ganesh signifies non-duality (only one tusk is left, that is consciousness, one without a second). The other reason he broke his tusk is to write the mahabharata. Ganesh is the God of Writers and enhances our intuitive writing abilities.

The large ears of Ganesh represent the ability to really listen and not merely hear. Many people hear and are thinking what to say next in their minds.

The large belly of Ganesh (Lambodhara) represents the ability to go beyond the opposites of life (duality) and realize the non-dual consciousness within us (intuitive self-realization). It also represents the fullness (Purna) of consciousness. He believes life is about perfecting while feeling perfect at every stage. In other words, we can always get better with a feeling of contentment and fullness at every moment.

The cobra wrapped around his belly represents the arousal of the dormant kundalini shakti within us. Ganesh lies at the muladhara chakra and guards the kundalini shakti (metaphorically he guards the cave of his mother Goddess Shakti who was taking a bath).

The ax Ganesh holds in one hand chops the pull that multiplicity has on our ego. His other hand holds the noose with which he pulls the ego into pure non-dual conscious, so enlightenment happens to your ego. We know who we are, pure unbounded consciousness.

To explain this further, Vedanta teaches us that our ego straddles a line between this world of duality and pure non-dual consciousness. This was actually one of the greatest teachings of Shankaracharya in his Adhyasa Bhashya of the Brahmasutras. The ego gets enmeshed in the world and we start basing our happiness on whether our desires are fulfilled in the world. The ax of Ganesha chops this pull and the noose he holds in the other hand pulls your ego home where it belongs, pure consciousness.

The Sanskrit word for ego is ahamkara (the 'I' maker) and the Sanskrit word for the vast nature of consciousness is maha. Interestingly, when Ganesh chops the pull of this world on our ego and flips it back, it is the same as flipping back aham and you get maha. Thus, the individual becomes the macrocosmic. That is why Ganesh has an elephant head on the human body. The elephant head represents maha and the human body is aham. Ganesh represents the great mahavakya (great saying) of the vedas: Tat tvam asi. (That thou art). It literally means you are infinite. The little known Ganapati

Upanishad (Ganesha Atharva Shirsha) elevates every aspect of Ganesha as symbols of consciousness and starts off with this mahavakya of tat tvam asi as an homage to Lord Ganesha.

DANCING SHIVA (Nataraja)
Mantra: Om Nama Shivaya

Summary: Nataraja is the archetype of anyone experiencing radical change in life, be it a new relationship, career, or a spiritual path. Shiva teaches us to embrace life with joy and a sense of wonder.

Life is uncertain. Anything can happen anytime to anyone of us. The real question is how does one live such a life of uncertainty with certainty?

The answer is to embrace the dancer, the Shiva Nataraja, the joyous dancer. Nata means the dance and Raja means king.

This is the dance of creation and destruction of the universe that each of us co-creates. The circle of flames represents the world we have created. Everything we experience is due to the karmas we have incurred from the past, including past lives.

The circle of flames represents our destiny coming from previous karmic patterns. We possess free will, which is represented by the flame Shiva holds in his hand. This is likened to the fire in the belly we need in order to transform and get out of our comfort zone.

On the other hand, Shiva holds the damaru, the drum or the beating pulse of creation. Time and space comes from this beat. The whole universe vibrates from the damaru of Lord Shiva.

The top two hands of Shiva symbolize creation in your life. However, when you engage in creating something new in your life, the old thoughts, patterns, and relationships drag you down. This is represented by the being of forgetfulness, Apasmra, under Shiva's feet. The word 'smra' comes from 'smriti,' which means to remember. For instance, the Bhagavad Gita is a smriti, a remembered text. 'Apasmra' means you literally forget, you get paralyzed by change, you get stuck in the same rut of life, you become like a deer caught in the headlights. Apasmra also represents the demons within us, the old ways of thinking, the old patterns (samskaras) and addictions that sometimes drag us down.

What Shiva does is to crush the back of Apasmra with his right foot and teach us that life is about creation and destruction, simultaneously.

Another conundrum we face during conscious change is that we worry about the results of our transformation. It comes from our ego, we remember the past mistakes we have made or become uncertain of the results of our transformation and feel what if it doesn't work out. It's very natural to feel this uncertainty and its part of the human experience.

To address this, Lord Shiva does two things. He raises his left foot and brings his left arm over to point to his raised left foot (sharanagati mudra). This literally means let it go, surrender as shown by Shiva's hand gesturing to one of his feet. The word surrender to an average person means giving up or losing something. To the yogi, surrender is like a drop of water merging with the ocean. You essentially gain the infinite. The individual drop is indistinguishable from the ocean and that's where the certainty in our lives comes in; when we realize that we are the ocean that is never born and never dies.

When we truly surrender, Shiva raises his right hand in the Abhaya mudra (blessing). This mudra means that he removes fears and uncertainties from within us. The entire yogic path is a combination of effort and grace. We do the effort, the sadhanas, the yogic practices to surrender and grace smiles at you.

Interestingly, when Lord Shiva points to his left leg with his left hand, he crosses his heart. The crossing of the heart represents the deepest, darkest moments in our lives (the proverbial dark night of the soul). This miserable time is actually an opportunity to surrender and exponential gains can come in your spiritual path. That is why in the Bhagavad Gita, Arjuna received the highest teachings from Lord Krishna when Arjuna was at his most despondent state.

Most of humanity lives on the circle of the wheel of samsara, as shown by the circular flames around Shiva. We are buffeted by waves of change, of creation, and destruction. Change is inevitable whether we seek it or not. By the time you are reading this, you are not the same person you were a second ago; thousands of cells in your body have died and thousands have been born. But, in a spinning wheel around Lord Shiva, something never changes. This is the center. If you look carefully at the murti of Nataraja, the center is where the heart is. This is the seat of pure consciousness, the 'I Am.'

The Upanishads talk about this pure consciousness residing in our heart space. Lord Shiva tells us that life is a dance, it's inherently chaotic, engage with it, create, destroy. Do not, however, make the dance into a drama. Know who you are, you are pure consciousness, the stillness that is never born nor dies.

The cobra represents desire because desire is like a cobra injecting its venom. When you get infected, it's very hard to remove it. Shiva is the ultimate yogi. He has desires, but the desires don't control him. He wears the cobra as an adornment, as a decoration, as jewelry, and even they are flying in the dance symbolizing that he is the master of desires.

Finally, just like the way the cobra sheds its skin representing transformation, Shiva's cobra represents the alchemy of transforming our desires into the highest desire for spiritual awakening. This is also represented as the three and a half coiled spring cobra that resides in our muladhara chakra. This Kundalini serpent energy uncoils through us upon kundalini awakening and rises up through all the seven chakras.

DURGA

Mantra: Om Dum Durga Yei Namah

Summary: Goddess Durga is goodness in a fierce form. She removes the negative energies that don't serve us both within as well as directed towards us.

There is always a story around which the philosophy is intertwined. There was this demon king, Mahishasura (mahish means buffalo and asura means demon). He meditated on Lord Shiva. Shiva gets easily pleased when you meditate or do puja on him. Shiva gave the demon a boon that no existing god or goddess could kill him, essentially the boon of immortality. A boon is nothing more than an intention coming to fruition. This demon symbolizes our deepest samskaras or ingrained patterns, which are seemingly immortal that no existing ego can vanquish. This is what results in addictions or stuff that holds us back from reaching our highest potential.

Mahishasura became arrogant and started to torture a lot of people, just like our deepest pattern tortures us over many lifetimes.

All the gods and goddesses then got together and essentially created a new entity, Maa Durga. Since she wasn't an existing deity, the boon didn't apply. Each of them gave an aspect of themselves to her so Durga is an amalgamation of all the gods and goddesses. Lord Ram gave the bow, Kali gave the ax, Hanuman gave the mace, Vishnu gave the discus and conch, Parvati Shakti gave the beautiful face, Lakshmi gave the lotus. This incredibly beautiful goddess comes riding on a fierce lion bobbing up and down. The demon king takes one look at her and falls in love. He tells her to marry him and they will torture the world together. She wouldn't have it and chopped his head off.

There is powerful symbolism in this story. The reason our ego is powerless to deal with these samskaras is because our ego is the subtlest aspect of the mind, which is a part of the subtle body. The samskaras are ingrained in our causal body. (That is why some of these samskaras come from earlier lifetimes.) Ego is like the proverbial flashlight, while these samskaras are like the battery controlling the flashlight; the flashlight tries to look for and control the battery, but it can't.

Durga as your archetype resides in your causal body, the same plane as these samskaras. She is able to kill the demons that plague us and clean out the patterns of repetitive behavior that hold us back by attenuating the effects of the samskaras that can lead to addictions. She gives us inner strength and outer compassion so you can help people while having an inner firmness. Durga is goodness in a fierce form.

The lion she rides is like a dream (swapna simhata) that pounces on you and frightens you awake and into a higher state.

LAKSHMI
Mantra: Om Shrim Maha Lakshmi Yei Namah

Summary: Lakshmi teaches us to embrace life with abundance both material and spiritual. She is also the goddess of Shri, that which gives you luminosity and enables to create beauty in every aspect of life.

Lakshmi holds lotuses in each hand because it represents purity or sattva. A lotus can bloom in mud or a dirty pond. Lakshmi says your true nature is like a Lotus and can bloom regardless of your surroundings. With her right hand, she does the abhaya mudra which is the palm facing out. This means protection and fearlessness where she removes fears and uncertainties within you on your way to abundance. With her left hand, she gives abundance and prosperity, the varada mudra. The abundance she grants you is universal abundance where everything in the universe is part of you. This signifies the tantric way of awakening where the realization dawns that everything is shri, this is the Pravritti path of expansion in tantra. Shri is the luminous quality some people have, the way they talk, the way they dress, the way they look, the way they do any job; there is a luminous glow about them. Even menial tasks are done with shri. I once saw someone clean the floor of a toilet with shri. Every moment in life, be it good or bad, is embraced wholeheartedly. This Pravritti path involves worldly duties; this is the path of awakening through the path of the grihastha or the householder yogi.

The worldly Goddess Lakshmi teaches us to be grihastha yogis, the path of the householder. She teaches us to bring the ashram home.

SARASWATI

Mantra: Om Eim Saraswati Yei Namah

Summary: Saraswati is the goddess of knowledge, speech, intuitive wisdom, music, dance, and creativity.

Saraswati literally means 'flow' because she was a river in ancient India 5,000 years ago where the Vedic civilization existed. Everything flows with her grace. Saraswati says the way to awakening is twofold. One way is through scripture, this is the path of Jnana, intellectual knowledge of the Vedas and the Agamas. The other path is through the heart represented by the large veena or the sitar. Chanting opens the heart chakra. Great insights can happen when the heart chakra is opened. In this age of kali yuga or darkness, where greed, jealousy, and wars dominate, the way of the heart is what she recommends.

The flow of intuition Saraswati grants you is of the highest kind (pashyanti vak) where you become so good at what you do that eloquence flows naturally from a source of deep wisdom. This flow leads to great creative advancements in knowledge, music, dance, and the arts.

Saraswati gives you the highest power of matrika shakti, the inherent creative energy behind the letters that make up words. Your words and teachings start to carry potent shakti or power. It is said that each letter of the Sanskrit alphabet has a corresponding sound vibration both in the subtle energy channels of our bodies and in the cosmos. When these sound vibrations resonate with a corresponding vibration within us they create thoughts, then these thoughts gradually manifest the grosser forms of feelings and then speech. This matrika shakti resides as the archetype of Maa Saraswati in our causal body and rises of its own volition into consciousness, manifesting as our thoughts.

The swan's head is shown on one end of the sitar. The swan metaphorically represents viveka, the key quality of discernment a spiritual seeker should possess. Just like the mythical swan is able to separate milk from water, the highest viveka enables one to separate reality from maya. The swan called Hamsa also glides gracefully through water without water sticking to it. Under the water, the swan scurries furiously. The great sages do sadhana (spiritual practice) in order to maintain their swan-like appearance.

BUDDHA
Mantra: Om Buddha Yei Namah

Summary: Buddha brings calm, peace of mind, and ultimate spiritual awakening. In addition, the medicine Buddha from the Tibetan tradition heals both the body and mind.

The Buddha, the deity for compassion, healing, and bringer of liberation. Buddha means the awakened one. He awoke from this living dream with enlightenment, and moksha (release from the cycle of birth and death). It comes from the root buddhi, the intellect. Thus, Buddha means the intellect has awakened to the self.

The buddhi is the closest mental faculty we have to the self. This is the main purpose of chanting the gayatri mantra from the Rig Veda:

Oṃ bhūr bhuvaḥ svaḥ
tát savitúr váreṇ(i)yaṃ
bhárgo devásya dhīmahi
dhíyo yó naḥ pracodáyāt

The dhi used in the 3ʳᵈ and 4ᵗʰ lines denote the buddhi. It means let the light of all lights, the light of consciousness illuminates the buddhi to awaken to the self.

The murti of Buddha has the jnana mudra where the forefinger forms a circle with his thumb. Forefinger is the ego as it represents our sense of individuality. We point at ourselves to take credit or at others to indicate it's their fault. Thumb represents the self because we always use the thumb for all tasks such as writing and lifting (and nowadays texting). The other four fingers are powerless without the thumb. Ego meets the self and forms a perfect circle that has no beginning or end, something changeless. This is enlightenment. Ego leaves behind three aspects associated with it—body, mind, and intellect. These are represented by the other three fingers.

The ears of Buddha are shown elongated representing inner detachment. Buddha was originally Prince Siddharta who used to wear heavy gold jewelry and left his worldly possessions to realize his Buddha nature.

TARA
Mantra: Oṃ Tāre Tuttāre Ture Svāhā

Summary: Tara is the goddess of compassion, healing, and bringer of people to liberation.

Going up the mountain for internal and external peace is a metaphor for the spiritual path. That is what Buddha did: he retreated from society, meditated, and went within. Buddha means the awakened one and doesn't reincarnate amongst us. However, Avalokiteswara, (the lord who looks down), the enlightened, feminine aspect of Buddha sheds tears upon seeing the suffering in this world of samsara. Motivated by great compassion she decides to reincarnate amongst us as bodhisattvas (enlightened beings).

Thus, beings such as Goddess Tara descend down the mountain into this world of chaos and uncertainty so they can help people with love, healing, and achieving moksha.

At the highest level, Tara continues to reincarnate until everyone gets awakened. Tara is similar to Kwan Yin in the sense they are both bodhisattvas. The difference is that Tara comes from a Nepal/Tibet/India tradition while Kwan-Yin comes from China and the Far East tradition.

In our daily lives, Tara appears as an archetype in people who are great healers and serve selflessly. Prominent examples are Mother Theresa and Mahatma Gandhi. The boddhisattvas never get tired because they are aligned with the divine energy. The tiredness comes when there is a selfish ego-based intention and when that is not met, the mind generates static. With Gandhi for instance, he couldn't be bought with money or political power and he had no selfish ego-based intentions. People sensed his genuineness and a billion people followed him. He altered world history along with the likes of Martin Luther King and Nelson Mandela who were inspired by him. That is the power of the boddhisattva, a living liberated who serves unconditionally by being aligned with the divine shakti.

Interestingly, Mahatma Gandhi was inspired by the essays on civil disobedience by Henry David Thoreau whose teacher was Ralph Waldo Emerson who in turn was profoundly inspired by the Bhagavad Gita.

KRISHNA
Mahamantra:

hare kṛṣṇa hare kṛṣṇa
kṛṣṇa kṛṣṇa hare hare

hare rāma hare rāma

rāma rāma hare hare

Summary: Krishna Radha is the archetype of the highest relationship where one sees the divine spirit as Shri Krishna in each other.

At the core of every person is a longing for love, both to receive it and give it. Unlike many systems of philosophy that attempt to subdivide reality, prema or love has no boundaries or divisions. The highest epitome of prema is felt through a relationship where the divinity is experienced so intensely that the overwhelming joyous nature of satchitananda reveals itself. This archetype of the highest relationship is represented as Radha-Krishna. Krishna means the intensely attractive one and Radha is the beloved. When you visit Vrindavan in India, the land where Lord Krishna grew up, people address each other as Radhe-Radhe. It's a bit disconcerting in the beginning to be called Radha but the realization dawns that we are all Radhas wanting to merge in the supreme bliss of love with Krishna. Our personal relationships need to be viewed therefore as a personification of Radha-Krishna. Most relationships based on body-mind chemistry or compatibility can be challenging to maintain in the long run because of the ever-changing nature of our bodies and minds. However, when the relationship is based on seeing the divinity, goodness, and auspiciousness (as Shri Krishna) in one another, it is everlasting and becomes a vehicle for the supreme bliss of awakening. Jai Radhe!

HANUMAN

Mantra: Om Anjaneya Namah

Summary: In a nutshell, Hanuman represents superhuman strength and superhuman intellect with a high degree of devotion. He resides in the heart chakra. If there is one deity who embodies bhakti, it is Lord Hanuman.

Hanuman is actually an incarnation of Shiva and Shakti. Shiva was meditating on Mount Kailash one day and came to a realization that he shared with his wife

Shakti. He said Lord Ram is the main ruler of the universe. His wife Shakti said, "What are you saying? You are the main man!" Lord Shiva replied, "No, things have changed. People are living too much in their head and excessive egotism has lead to divisiveness, jealousy, wars, etc. So I'm going to incarnate as a lowly monkey so people will take me for granted. Through my selfless service, I'm going to show everyone the power of devotion and living from the heart." Shakti replied, "In that case, I'm going to incarnate as your tail so we will always be together." So Hanuman is Shiva and his tail represents the Kundalini Shakti. The word Shakti also means power and that's how he lights fire to the entire island of Lanka in the great epic of Ramayana.

Hanuman carries a mace that represents his weapon that he clubs the demons with. It is akin to the hammer Thor wields (but Hanuman is way smarter). Hanuman is the ultimate superhero. Many aspects of yoga come from Hanuman, including many asanas. He taught the yogic world pranayama because his faather was Vayu. He taught the world surya namaskar or sun salutation because his guru was Surya, the sun god. He is so intelligent that he is able to reconcile the three main systems of vedanta philosophy: dwaita (duality), vishishta advaita (qualified non-duality), and advaita (non-duality).

This is best illustrated in this story:
When this unassuming monkey becomes a superstar of the Ramayana, at the end Ram asks Hanuman "Who are you?"

Hanuman replies:

deha bhavena dasosmi - when I take identification with my body, I am your (God's) servant. This is Dwaita, duality where you are separate from God and thus express devotion, the path of Bhakti.

jiva bhavena twadamshakaha - when I take identification with the traveling soul, I am a part of you - this is Vishishta Advaita, qualified non duality where you are part of God.

Atma bhavena twamevaham - when I take identification with pure Consciousness, I am You - this is Advaita, pure non duality.

Saying this, Hanuman ripped his heart to reveal his Ishtadevata, Lord Ram.

KALI
Mantra: Om Kleeem Maha Kali Yei Namah

Summary: Goddess Kali as an archetype completely transforms your life. She is goodness in a fierce form. She removes the negative energies that don't serve us both within as well as directed towards us. Ultimately, Ma Kali leads us to enlightenment. The great sage Ramakrishna Parmahansa tried very hard to get moksha and finally he surrendered to Ma Kali. In one stroke she granted him liberation.

There was this demon king Rakta Bija. Rakta means blood and Bija means seed so Rakta Bija means seeds of blood. This demon meditated on Lord Shiva and Shiva gave the demon a boon that whenever a drop of blood falls on the ground, another clone is created. Essentially, it is the boon of immortality.

This demon Rakta Bija then becomes arrogant and starts to torture a lot of people, just like our deepest pattern tortures us over many lifetimes.

People got very worried about the imbalance on earth, the imbalance of our lives. So they went to Lord Shiva and asked him to help them. Shiva said, I'm too busy meditating, go bother my wife Shakti. So, they all went to Goddess Shakti. Shakti tells them I can help you. She manifested as a fierce, naked, dark Goddess Kali. Kali is a form of Shakti, Shiva's wife. She is naked because Maya (the world of illusion) doesn't cover her. She is dark, the nearest there is to pure consciousness.

Kali chops off the hands of the demons and makes a skirt. Her hands represent karmic actions and she removes the effects of karma that bind us. She chops off all the heads of the demon clones and makes a garland. This way she eliminates all the negative patterns (samskaras) that bind us down. There are 54 skulls in the garland representing 54 letters of the sanskrit alphabet. These skulls represent the samskaras, the addictive patterns that demonize our lives. Finally, she chops off the head of the main demon and sticks a bowl underneath so the blood doesn't spill anymore. The head of the main demon represents Avidya, ignorance of our true nature. Avidya created all the demonic samskaras and

Kali Maa grants us liberation from Avidya (ignorance or bondage) that leads to transmigration of souls.

But, the blood thirsty Goddess Kali wouldn't stop and she stomps around chanting, "I want more blood!" People get really worried because the earth starts to shake because of Kali Ma's ferocity. Everyone rushes to Lord Shiva. Instead of reasoning with Maa Kali, Shiva lays down in front of her. She steps on him, realizes it's her husband and cools down by sticking her tongue out. It's a classic pose in yoga to cool down. (Dogs do this instinctively.)

There is powerful symbolism here. Shiva represents the witnessing consciousness within us (the 'I Am'). Shakti means the power of consciousness. You can never reach Shiva, the subjective consciousness. You can never talk nor think about it because it is the eternal subject. You arrive at your Shiva nature by working with Kali. Kali is Shiva Shakti!

Goddess Kali cleans out the patterns of repetitive behavior that holds us back. She cleans out the samskaras that can lead to addictions. She gives us inner strength and outer compassion to help people while having an inner firmness. Maa Kali is goodness in a fierce form.

MOKSHA TANDAVA (Dance of Ultimate Freedom)
Mantra: Om Namah Shivaya

Summary: It is the dance of an enlightened being, the culmination of all spiritual paths.

This rare murti is Shiva dancing the ultimate dance of a liberated being, the moksha tandava. When he dances as Nataraja, he is called Ananda Tandava. Tandava means dance and Ananda is joy. Nataraja is the dance of the joy of embodiment. There are 108 poses in the dance and the final pose is Shiva upside down doing the one handed bent handstand. You need to first understand Nataraja and then the moksha tandava because the dance of ultimate freedom comes directly from being able to live in this world of uncertainty with certainty. A key element of these practices is that they lead to chitthashuddhi.

All the yogic sadhanas (practices) you do—meditation, chanting, karma yoga, etc.—are designed for chitthashuddhi (purifying the mind). It is like cleaning the dust off the mirror of our mind. The sun is always shining, however, when the mirror of the mind metaphorically has dust, it's difficult to see the light of pure consciousness. We have had millions of incarnations that can leave a heavy coating in the mirror of our mind. The yogic practices are designed to purify the mind for the highest teachings of jnana (self-knowledge) that leads to freedom or moksha.

This freedom comes from the flame Lord Shiva holds in one hand. It represents the fire of jnana, where all lifetimes of darkness are lit up with the fire of knowledge. The Latin word video (to see) comes from the sanskrit vidya (knowledge). Avidya means we are ignorant of our true nature as unconditioned consciousness. Lifetimes of Avidya are dissipated with a single source of illuminative wisdom.

The hand going back on Shiva represents ultimate freedom. The damaru (drum) Shiva holds in the other hand means that time and space come from within. One side of the drum is this world of multiplicity whereas the other side represents pure non-dual consciousness, the self, the 'I Am.' In other words, the universe comes from within you.

A spontaneous alchemy of transformation happens where the legs go up and the hands go down. All sense of doer-ship is gone in this state. When you do a handstand in yoga, the muscles of your hands and legs are contorted with stress. In moksha tandava, it is just effortless grace because you realize that nobody really does anything. The main aspect of enlightenment is that the sense of doer-ship is gone. There is no up, no down. Everything is Shiva, the divine auspicious consciousness.

The apasmara under Lord Shiva's foot represents the old karmic patterns that still need to be exhausted. These prarabdha karmas are always there giving rise to our embodiment, it's like a fan being switched off, it takes a while before coming to a stop. Lord Shiva managing these prarabdha karmas with his hand represents the sadhanas (spiritual practices) one must do to maintain these karmas. For instance, one of the great sages of the last century, Ramana Maharshi, had throat cancer after enlightenment. He never felt the pain because of his sadhanas. It's like the famous Zen saying, after enlightenment one still chops wood, carries water, and does the dishes.

The Upanishads talk about moksha samsaraat, which means the cessation of all suffering. It means you may have desires but you do not base your happiness on the fulfillment of external desires. That is because your true nature is joy. Moksha means you have discovered your true nature.

ADDITIONAL RESEARCH
AND ARTICLES OF INTEREST

Phyllis Moen is a Sociologist. She became a widow at a young age and had to raise her children as a single working parent. She dedicated years of her life researching, writing, and teaching about the ideal balance that brings fulfillment in work and in life. She set out to debunk implied societal rules and expectations.

It is tough to work full-time while raising a family as a single parent. While I did not raise my children as a single parent like Phyllis, I did work throughout my children's lives (still do), my husband worked long hours and was unable to be home until well after the children's bedtime most nights, and one of my three is disabled. So, I can identify with Phyllis.

We all have challenges and we often suffer in silence, while dreaming of what the right work/life balance is for us and how we can pursue our passion with happiness as our ultimate goal. Phyllis dedicated her life to studying the dilemma of finding this balance. In a way, like Phyllis, I did too.

In *Beyond the Career Mystique*, *"Time In," "Time Out,"* and *"Second Acts,"* Phyllis talks about the career mystique in our society:

The career mystique embraces both an endurance ethic and a work ethic, both crucial to American values of individualism and free enterprise. "Sacrifice by working hard," the myth goes, and you'll reap wealth, security, status, health insurance, pensions, respect, love, admiration, happiness, and, eventually, the leisure of a retirement without financial worries. The obverse is also true: If success is deserved, the product of a lifetime of hard work, so too is failure. In other words, the career mystique implies that those who don't "make it" simply do not try hard enough.

Throughout my years in corporate America and executive recruiting, I have learned that happiness is not directly related to hard work. In fact, it is the effortless pursuit of our passions, where work seems like play and time is irrelevant, that brings us ultimate fulfillment, meaning, and happiness in our lives. I think Phyllis would agree. Maybe we shouldn't try so hard. Rather, find ways to be happy in each moment of each day. When we put ourselves in a state of happiness, it is amazing how things start to fall into place for us.

———◈———

According to an article in *Psychology Today* by Dr. Todd Kashdan:

- One's purpose cannot be another's goals; purpose is at the highest level of analysis in defining a person's identity.
- A purpose in life ought to stimulate behavioral consistency; serving as the motivating force to overcome obstacles, seek alternative means, and maintain focus on the goal in spite of changes to the environment that may interfere with the pursuit.
- One of the beautiful things in science is that every study leads to more questions. There are some interesting, lingering issues when it comes to understanding, developing, and benefitting from a purpose in life.

———◈———

In an article by Cathy Caprino for *Forbes*, she explores the connection between happiness and success. She interviews Shawn Achor who gave a TED Talk on the Happy Secret to Better Work. (You can find a link to his talk in the resources section of *SHIFT*.) His talk has received more than 4 million views, and it's not because he teaches at Harvard. Shawn's talk supports what I have been saying all along: when we are happy, good things happen.

Cathy asked Shawn how we can increase happy experiences and this is what he told her:

- **Bring gratitude to mind** – Write down three new things that you are grateful for each day.
- **Journal** – Journal about a positive experience you've had recently for two minutes once a day.

- **Exercise** – Engage in 15 minutes of mindful cardio activity.
- **Meditate** – Watch your breath go in and out for two minutes a day.
- **Engage in a random, conscious acts of kindness** – Write a two-minute positive email thanking a friend or colleague, or compliment someone you admire on social media.

Do these steps for 21 days and you will begin to see a lasting shift in your mindset towards more positivity.

Be sure to listen to his TED Talk. He is funny and you will ponder your own happiness.

A *New York Times* opinion article in 2015 about rethinking work sited a Gallup Poll report claiming that nine out of 10 employees are dissatisfied at work. According to the article, when given the chance to make their work meaningful and engaging, employees jump at it, even if it means that they have to work harder.

Companies have started to pay attention and, the good news is, the numbers are up.

According to a 2016 report in the *Wall Street Journal*, employee job satisfaction is at a 10-year high, but still below 50 percent. That sounds great since it's better than only 10 percent of workers experiencing satisfaction. Yet, what we need to realize is that close to 50 percent is a far cry from 100 percent.

We still have work to do.

Employee engagement can lead to increased satisfaction at work and, if we become more creative in the way we value and reward our employees, I think we can get that number way up. When employees are happy, they work harder. I know this because I speak with unhappy and happy employees every day. The difference in focus, dedication, and output is staggering.

Feeling valued can directly affect morale and relate to success for companies. I know a company who is instituting two-month sabbaticals between promotions from Associate to Vice President for example. The Managing Director of one of the company offices told me that the employee would receive full salary during the sabbatical and be encouraged to do something they have always wanted to do. Sail, climb a mountain, meditate, travel, learn a new hobby; whatever they wanted. The idea is to clear their head for the next stage in their career. This is similar to Virgin and Netflix who don't really count vacation days and they have a high level of employee productivity.

Additionally, allowing employees to have control over decisions and innovate can be very effective.

At C2C, we focus on employee engagement as well as executive recruiting. In reading this book, you may be shifting in your career or you may be a company who wants employees to shift in the direction of staying or becoming more engaged. In order to do so, you must think outside of your current corporate parameters and let the sky be your limit.

———◆———

From my professional experience and perspective, finding true meaning in work and life is all about happiness.

The end goal is happiness. The beginning goal is happiness, too.

Feeling good, looking for the good signs, will beget good. Life will be easy, success will come and you will have a blast along the way.

It's not the other way around. We don't need to work harder, find success and happiness will follow.

If you don't believe everything I have shared in this book, just look into the many articles/books/talks that I have sited and reread the stories of the amazing people in *SHIFT* who have found true meaning in their work and in their lives through shifts. In the end, they all have one thing in common: happiness.

———◆———

The underlying secret in *SHIFT* is nothing more than happiness.

Be happy right now in this moment, and the next, and the next, and the next. Your life will blossom in ways you never imagined.

Once you achieve happiness, you have found success, which is really a function of improving the lives of oneself and others by what you do, the relationships you foster, and the legacy you leave.

Go after your dreams, find happiness, and create a beautiful legacy. I am excited for your journey!

Questions And Practices To Consider

- What are you passionate about?
- What is holding you back from pursuing your passion?
- If you have one year to live, write down three things you would absolutely want to do or feel before you go.
- Can you do one thing today that gets you closer to one of those things on your list?
- What is the one thing you would tell your closest friend that is true to your heart?
- How do you feel after being completely honest and vulnerable?
- Do you know what your dream job is? List the five jobs you would love to have no matter how outrageous or seemingly impossible they may seem.
- Can you list the first three things that you can do to move toward the job at the top of that list?
- What is your ideal romantic relationship?
- Brainstorm alone or as a group one thing you can do to get a little closer to that dream.
- What is the best advice you have ever been given? Does the advice make you feel good?
- Empty your mind. Sit in silence for five minutes. What comes up for you? Let the thoughts come and go. Do you experience more clarity on any particular topic that you desire? Great ideas come when we empty our minds.
- Do you believe in yourself? What is a positive affirmation you can say to yourself every morning when you wake up?
- Think of a good thought and share it with your group or a friend. Does it make you happy to share these thoughts? Think of another good thought. When you bring struggles into your thoughts after this

exercise, be kind to yourself. Try saying things like, I am getting better at that, I am figuring it out, I am getting there. You will be amazed what good things come into your life when you are feeling good about you.

• Many shifts are experienced by what may seem like chance, circumstance, or coincidence. We need to see the opportunities and signs and choose a direction at the fork in the road. What elements of serendipity have you experienced and have you or have you not moved in a certain direction because of them?

• No one can make you happy in work and life. Your journey is up to you. You have to take care of you first. Have you ever put the pressure aside for a moment to celebrate you? The world will follow your lead and fill in the blanks so that you can realize your deepest desires in work and in life.

NOTES

RESOURCES

Introduction

1. http://www.gallup.com/poll/181289/majority-employees-not-engaged-despite-gains-2014.aspx
2. Carmine Gallo (2014). Talk Like TED: The 9 Public Speaking Secrets of the World's Top Minds: Macmillan. 288.

PART ONE: WHY SHIFT?

3. http://bit.ly/1MEzsQ8
4. http://www.amazon.com/Psycho-Cybernetics-New-More-Living-Life/dp/0671700758
5. https://uwaterloo.ca/find-out-more/applicants/waterloo-contests

Chapter 1: Shift Happens

Photos: ifoster.com Serita Cox — Co–Founder/iFoster.org/Reid Cox — Co-Founder

6. http://www.ifoster.org
7. https://www.fosterclub.com/article/what-foster-care

8. http://bit.ly/2aFg97T
9. https://en.wikipedia.org/wiki/Mark_Wahlberg
10. http://bit.ly/2aJDyES
11. http://www.drjoecarver.com/clients/49355/File/Emotional%20 Memory.html
12. http://www.businessinsider.com/bre-x-6-billion-gold-fraud-indonesia-2012-7
13. 4http://www.socialimpactatbain.com/leave-a-legacy/sector-innovation/bridgespan.aspx
14. http://www.hhs.gov/hipaa/for-individuals/guidance-materials-for-consumers/index.html
15. http://www.linkedin.com; http://www.apple.com; http://www.google.com; http://www.zappos.com
16. https://www.gpo.gov/fdsys/pkg/CREC-2016-04-29/pdf/CREC-2016-04-29-pt1-PgE630-4.pdf#page=1
17. Isaacson, W (2015). Steve Jobs: The Exclusive Biography. USA: Abacus. 592.

Chapter 2: Against The Odds

18. http://jco.ascopubs.org/content/28/5/872.full
19. http://kidshealth.org/en/parents/self-esteem.html
20. http://www.telegraph.co.uk/news/health/news/8662822/Childhood-illness-harms-career-prospects.html
21. http://www.cancer.gov/about-cancer/coping/survivorship/new-normal/ptsd-pdq
22. http://www.ncbi.nlm.nih.gov/pmc/articles/PMC2811161/
23. https://en.wikipedia.org/wiki/Vaginoplasty
24. http://www.businessinsider.com/ceo-learning-disabilities-2011-5#richard-bransons-dyslexia-made-high-school-especially-difficult-1
25. https://en.wikipedia.org/wiki/Stephen_Hawking
26. https://www.verywell.com/celebrity-parents-of-children-with-special-needs-3105866

27. https://www.verywell.com/what-is-angelman-syndrome-3105636
28. http://greatergood.berkeley.edu/article/item/can_suffering_lead_to_success
29. https://www.amazon.com/gp/product/006226785X/ref=as_li_tl?ie=UTF8&camp=1789&creative=390957&crea tiveASIN=006226785X&linkCode=as2&tag=gregooscicen-20&linkId=X32YJGUBYXZBL3HZ
30. http://www.imdb.com/name/nm0115537/
31. http://www.cancer.org/cancer/ovariancancer/detailedguide/ovarian-cancer-detection
32. https://www.mskcc.org/cancer-care/patient-education/total-pelvic-exenteration
33. https://www.gofundme.com/

Chapter 3: Simplicity

34. Photos: On location by J.B. Miller - Achuar Chief
35. https://en.wikipedia.org/wiki/Shamanism
36. http://www.pachamama.org (organization for the support of the indigenous tribes of the Amazon Rain Forest
37. https://en.wiktionary.org/wiki/natem
38. https://en.wikipedia.org/wiki/Ciprofloxacin
39. http://www.nytimes.com/2010/10/17/travel/17Ecuador.html?_r=0
40. https://en.wikipedia.org/wiki/Amazon_river_dolphin
41. http://www.worldwildlife.org/blogs/good-nature-travel/posts/five-myths-about-amazon-river-dolphins
42. http://www.scientificamerican.com/article/why-we-are-wired-to-connect/https://en.wikipedia.org/wiki/Chicha
43. https://en.wikipedia.org/wiki/Ayahuasca
44. http://www.ayahuasca-info.com/introduction/
45. http://www.mintpressnews.com/213663-2/213663/

PART TWO: WHEN TO SHIFT

Chapter 4: Finding Normal

46. http://www.metrolyrics.com/just-breathe-lyrics-pearljam.
47. http://www.cbsnews.com/news/60-minutes-going-to-extremes/
48. http://www.amazon.com/Life-After-Investigation-Phenomenon-Survival-Bodily/dp/0062517392
49. http://www.rogerebert.com/reviews/buck-2011
50. http://www.rogerebert.com/reviews/the-horse-whisperer-1998
51. http://www.moonshineink.com/news/squaw-pro-skier-timy-dutton-dead-after-skydiving-accident
52. http://www.mensjournal.com/magazine/shane-mcconkeys-last-run-20131031
53. http://money.cnn.com/2015/09/28/media/erik-roner-dead/
54. https://en.wikipedia.org/wiki/SEAL_Team_Six
55. http://taskandpurpose.com/truth-22-veteran-suicides-day/

Chapter 5: Alleviate Suffering

56. https://en.wikipedia.org/wiki/Jerry_Colonna_(financier)
57. https://en.wikipedia.org/wiki/Silicon_Alley
58. https://www.crunchbase.com/organization/flatiron-partners#/entity
59. https://www.biblegateway.com/passage/?search=Acts+9
60. https://www.amazon.com/Let-Your-Life-Speak
61. Listeningdp/0787947350?ie=UTF8&hvadid=32507218231&hvdev=c&hvexid=&hvnetw=g&hvpone=&hvpos=1t2&hvptwo=&hvqmt=b&hvrand=7777287940273492677&ref=pd_sl_56yhrmimkf_b&tag=googhydr-20
62. https://www.counseling.org/docs/disaster-and-trauma_sexual-abuse/long-term-effects-of-childhood-sexual-abuse.pdf?sfvrsn=2
63. http://ct.counseling.org/2014/06/the-toll-of-childhood-trauma/
64. https://www.reboot.io/

65. http://avc.com/2012/02/the-management-team-guest-post-by-jerry-colonna/
66. https://www.reboot.io/podcast/
67. https://www.globalgiving.org/donate/24422/tibetan-village-project/info/
68. http://www.iep.utm.edu/buddha/

PART THREE: HOW TO SHIFT

Chapter 6: Overcoming Obstacles

69. http://www.accademia.org/explore-museum/artworks/michelangelos-david/
70. http://www.aaa.si.edu/collections/interviews/oral-history-interview-monty-lewis-12016
71. http://www.foodnetwork.com/chefs/giada-de-laurentiis.html
72. http://www.giadadelaurentiis.com/vegas/

Chapter 7: Faith Beyond Reason

73. http://www.sparknotes.com/lit/oldtestament/section11.rhtml
74. http://www.ncbi.nlm.nih.gov/pmc/articles/PMC1697747/
75. http://familyaware.org/expert-profiles/dr-carol-glod-teen-depression.html
76. http://biblehub.com/romans/9-8.htm
77. http://www.biblestudy.org/bibleref/meaning-of-numbers-in-bible/4.html
78. https://www.amazon.com/Parenting-Inside-Out-Self-Understanding-
79. http://www.ncbi.nlm.nih.gov/pmc/articles/PMC486942/
80. http://www.mayoclinic.org/diseases-conditions/chronic-fatigue-syndrome/basics/symptoms/con-20022009
81. http://www.tinabryson.com/#home-page
82. https://www.mindsightinstitute.com/

Chapter 8: Synchronicity

Photos: Manoj and Jyothi Chalam – provided by Manoj

83. Jung, C (2002). The Undiscovered Self. UK: Routledge. 79
84. http://www.wsj.com/articles/why-americas-top-technology-jobs-are-going-to-indian-executives-1439338706
85. http://www.forbes.com/sites/singularity/2012/10/15/how-indians-defied-gravity-and-achieved-success-in-silicon-valley/#4b03b5176d1e
86. https://dattatreyasivababamiracles.wordpress.com/archetypes-2/
87. "The Psychology of the Child Archetype," CW 9i, par. 284, The Collected Works of Carl Jung
88. http://vedanta.org/vedanta-overview/
89. http://www.nytimes.com/1999/11/07/education/in-theory-the-teachings-of-carl-jung.html?pagewanted=all
90. http://www.khoslaventures.com/
91. https://www.amazon.com/Autobiography-Yogi-P-Yogananda/dp/8120725247
92. http://www.yogananda-srf.org/paramahansa_yogananda.aspx#.V2SPkuYrLGI
93. http://www.deepakchopra.com
94. https://en.wikipedia.org/wiki/Carl_Jung
95. https://en.wikipedia.org/wiki/Joseph_Campbell
96. https://en.wikipedia.org/wiki/Vaitheeswaran_Koil
97. https://en.wikipedia.org/wiki/Nadi_astrology
98. http://www.investopedia.com/university/ipo/ipo.asp
99. http://www.Vivekodayam.org
100. http://www.gatesfoundation.org/
101. https://en.wikipedia.org/wiki/Jimmy_Iovine
102. https://en.wikipedia.org/wiki/Dr._Dre
103. https://news.usc.edu/50816/jimmy-iovine-and-dr-dre-give-70-million-to-create-new-academy-at-usc/
104. https://www.youtube.com/watch?v=jSxEGIzq2Lk
105. http://givingpledge.org/index.html

106. http://www.thebestschools.org/features/most-generous-alumni-donors/
107. http://www.specialed.org/
108. http://www.pachamama.org/about/team
109. http://www.usatoday.com/story/sports/nfl/patriots/2015/02/02/tom-brady-super-bowl-four-seattle-seahawks-joe-montana/22729895/
110. https://www.youtube.com/watch?v=nL_m5X-YaHM
111. http://www.uniqueartsintl.com/
112. http://www.uniqueartsintl.com/

PART FOUR: AFTER THE SHIFT
113. http://robertwaldinger.com/

Now What?
114. https://www2.warwick.ac.uk/newsandevents/pressreleases/new_study_shows/
115. http://books.simonandschuster.com/Paris-A-Love-Story/Kati-Marton/9781451691559
116. https://en.wikipedia.org/wiki/Six_degrees_of_separation
117. https://www.psychologytoday.com/blog/curious/201502/what-do-scientists-know-about-finding-purpose-in-life
118. https://www.psychologytoday.com/blog/curious/201502/what-do-scientists-know-about-finding-purpose-in-life

Appendix
119. http://www.kashgar.com.au/articles/ganesh
120. https://www.pinterest.com/pin/551128073123500388/
121. http://sacredhinduism.com/hindu-goddess-durga-maa-pictures/
122. http://sacreddestinations.org/lakshmi-abundance-ritual-goddess-gathering-bristol.html
123. http://empiindia.com/blog/10-interesting-facts-about-goddess-saraswati/
124. http://www.johnworldpeace.com/budjesus.asp

125. http://www.mother-god.com/goddess-tara.html

126. http://aumamen.com/story/pride-of-a-radha-disciple

127. http://www.atozpictures.com/hanuman-pictures

128. https://www.google.com/search?q=KALI+HINDU+GODDESS& source=lnms&tbm=isch&sa=X&ved=0ahUKEwjGy7GJoqTOAhU H0WMKHU6aCJgQ_AUICCgB&biw=1122&bih=718#imgrc= Hz4w3E08eJsbRM%3A

129. https://www.google.com/search?q=KALI+HINDU+GODDESS& source=lnms&tbm=isch&sa=X&ved=0ahUKEwjGy7GJoqTOAhU H0WMKHU6aCJgQ_AUICCgB&biw=1122&bih=718 - imgrc= Hz4w3E08eJsbRM%3A

Additional Research And Articles Of Interest

130. http://users.soc.umn.edu/~moen/Research.htm

131. Moen, Phyllis. 2005. "Beyond the Career Mystique: "Time in," "Time Out," and "Second Acts"." *Sociological Forum* 20:187-208.

132. http://www.forbes.com/sites/kathycaprino/2013/06/06/how-happiness-directly-impacts-your-success/#622947ce7ae2

133. http://www.ted.com/talks/shawn_achor_the_happy_secret_to_better_work

134. http://www.nytimes.com/2015/08/30/opinion/sunday/rethinking-work.html?_r=0

135. http://www.wsj.com/articles/job-satisfaction-hits-a-10-year-highbut-its-still-below-50-1468940401

136. https://www.virgin.com/richard-branson/why-were-letting-virgin-staff-take-as-much-holiday-as-they-want

Notes: Questions And Practices To Consider

137. http://thedailyquotes.com/tag/work-life-balance/

138. http://www.brainyquote.com

139. http://www.inspirationboost.com

140. http://www.quotesgram.com

141. http://www.quoteslike.com

142. http://www.quotesgardentelugu.in/
143. http://www.keepinspiringme.com
144. http://www.keepinspiringme.com/

Samples Of Jody's Huffington Post Blog

145. https://en.wikipedia.org/wiki/Schadenfreude
146. http://www.teamintraining.org/
147. http://www.c2cexecutivesearch.com
148. http://www.huffingtonpost.com/jody-b-miller/your-key-employees-want-t_b_9865572.html
149. http://web.mit.edu/comm-forum/mit4/papers/Kiernan.pdf
150. http://www.rogerknapp.com/inspire/lincoln.htm
151. http://www.gatesfoundation.org/What-We-Do/Global-Development/Polio
152. https://www.getabstract.com/en/summary/leadership-and-management/a-curious-mind/24305
153. http://www.biography.com/people/muhammad-ali-9181165#synopsis
154. http://www.medicinenet.com/cauliflower_ear/article.htm
155. https://en.wikipedia.org/wiki/Shaun_Tomson
156. http://www.esalen.org/http://www.esalen.org/

About The Author

157. www.c2cexecutivesearch.com
158. http://www.specialed.org/
159. https://www.linkedin.com/in/hiredsecrets?trk=hp-identity-name
160. http://www.huffingtonpost.com/author/jmiller-253
161. http://www.ignites.com/

THE BALANCE OF
WORK AND PLAY

I grew up in a small town in New Jersey. Madison was maybe two miles long. I loved Christmas time on our dead end street. All of the neighbors would show up at the circle of grass at the end of our block, sing Christmas carols around a huge bonfire, consume too much sugar, and throw snowballs. It was simple and safe.

In the summertime, a group of us hooligans would get up before sunrise, throw pebbles at the windows of our friends (or pull on strings deep sleep friends would tie on their fingers the night before and dangle out of their windows), jump on our bikes, and ride to the local grade school's grassy hill to watch the sunrise. Why? Because we didn't have a care in the world.

It was innocent. It was fun.

And then we grew up.

Growing up is complicated. We enter the rat race, the road to some future success, yet we really have no idea where we are going.

We try to do well in school, get into the best college (that our parents can brag about), make money, get married, buy a house, start a family, go into debt, go on vacations (that we can brag about), and sock away for retirement.

What happened to hide-and-go-seek, putting on carnivals, dancing all night, and running through the cemetery screaming, "Ghost!" What happened to us?

I used to do synchronized swimming. I was dressed as a lobster in a piece called "*Cats and Rabbits.*" I loved it. I didn't care what anyone thought of me.

And then I did.

I'm not saying that this is bad, this growing up thing. I know we can't always just blow with the wind, but I do believe that, as we dive into our career journeys, we need to maintain a sense of joy in our work and personal lives in order to find true happiness throughout our time on earth.

I recently had a friend visit from Madison. A friend I have known since age 5 and who grew up on the next block. He and I sat at the bar at The Fairmont Hotel in San Francisco for hours, reminiscing about our youth and the fun times we had.

Our first concert together at Madison Square Garden at only 13 years old, throwing the football in his front yard (his youngest brother ended up going pro), the fun parties and dances, becoming state champs in football, and how the New York City *Village Voice* newspaper printed a picture of me on the foldout, staying out all night with friends just because...

Then, we shifted to our work, our goals for the future, and how we might pool our years of experience to do some projects together.

While both dimensions of our conversation were delightful, upon reflection, what meant the most to me was our history. The fact that we knew one another so well and that we could bounce around from personal to professional with ease.

"*Do you remember so and so?*"

"*Oh my gosh. I haven't heard that name in years.*"

"Well, he ended up in jail after a police standoff."

"Oh my god!"

"And so and so? What happened to her?"

"She runs a school for boys and adopted two kids. I always had a crush on her."

"I always had a crush on so and so."

"So let's talk about how we're going to form an alliance with group X so that we can help more companies thrive."

And on it went, flowing seamlessly from memories and laughter into a few business deals to consider.

Connection. History. Flow.

My friend and his brothers used to trick-or-treat around the neighborhood and then change masks and do it all over again. Mischief Night (the night before Halloween) was big in Jersey. It was when we got in a bit of innocent trouble, like ringing someone's doorbell and running, or putting toilet paper all over a tree in front of someone's house that you had a crush on…or didn't. They had to guess.

When it comes to our work, I believe it is important to inject some carefree fun into our day. We were all kids and if we don't keep some of our childlike nature, we end up being old before our time, and unhappy.

In the book, *Drive: The Surprising Truth About What Motivates Us* by Daniel Pink, we learn about research related to human motivation. In his book he talks about bringing fun into the workplace in order to improve the bottom line and engage employees, but we all don't work at companies like Apple, Google, or Zappos.

If your place of employment is more boring than waiting for a webpage to load with slow Wi-Fi, you might have to take matters into your own hands.

Here are a few things you can do to bring a little balance into your responsible adult work life.:

- Join a volleyball or softball team after work.
- Learn to surf.
- Join Team in Training and run your first marathon.
- Try meditation.
- Learn to paint or cook or play an instrument.
- Join a book group.

What I'm trying to say is seek out some fun.

Connecting with old friends, sharing laughter and memories is another way of injecting joy in your life. Facebook, Twitter, LinkedIn, Google and other social media give us the opportunity to connect in an instant. Do it.

The next time you go into that Monday morning meeting, you just might have a new little jig in your step.

HOW TO DEAL WITH THE COMPLAINERS IN YOUR LIFE

I know people who complain…a lot!

I can't stand it. Okay, I'm complaining about the complainers.

I have tried by offering potential solutions, strategies, and ways to make them feel better because when we feel good, good comes our way.

But, they won't have it. They complain for the sake of complaining. To feel bad not good and, to try to bring everyone and anyone who listens along for the ride, so that they can feel better.

Schadenfreude is a character trait wherein a person finds pleasure in other people's misery. It's an awful approach to life. I know several people like this and they are complainers, too. Making yourself feel better does not reside in glory over another's demise and then complaining about them because of their misery.

Making yourself feel better is simple: make yourself feel better. You are ultimately responsible for you, so you might as well seek out how to feel good. When we feel good, we attract good things, which makes us feel better and attract more good things. Get it?

The complainer often has other hitchhiking traits that add to their complaining characteristic and self-absorbed misery. They feel better when they express how they know so much more than everyone else.

Have you ever shared a new and exciting experience or inspiring piece of information you just learned with a complaining know it all? Do they respond by saying, "*Oh, I know all about that*" or "*I did that too and, by the way, it's not all it's cracked up to be.*"

You feel deflated, less than who you thought you were, and you are smack in the middle of their misery funnel. Stop sharing. They will shut you down. They want you to be miserable, to not enjoy life because they do not. To keep you from passing them by, they want to bring you along on their ride to nowhere.

They may be smarter, more talented, and have a lot to offer the world, yet they sit in their home all day complaining. Did I mention that I cannot stand it? I think that complaining, arrogant, judgmental, and a know-it-all attitudes are lethal to happiness.

So what brings happiness?

Happiness.

How do you achieve happiness? Think good things, not bad. Do something that makes you feel good, not bad.

The first and most important way to get on the path to happiness is to stop complaining. Just stop. No one wants to you hear it, no one wants to be around it, and, if you keep doing it, it will become part of your DNA. Soon you will find yourself all alone because people can't stand complainers. Who wants to be around someone who has complained about being in constant pain for the past 10 years? Who wants to hear that everyone is an idiot: the doctors, the system, the junk mail senders, the computer (which is a person to complainers), the lady next door?

If you have someone like this in your life, here are some approaches to take:

- **Listen. Let them vent and then leave.**
- **Make the visits shorter and shorter.**
- **Stop offering solutions, strategies, options; stop trying to help. They really don't want it. They just want to complain.**

- **Don't start complaining!**
- **Give them all of your money, time, energy. They will stop complaining for a while, but they** *will* **start again. So maybe save a little for yourself.**

People like this have such aversion to happiness; they are only comfortable in misery. You can't help these people. You are not a professional. I don't even know if a professional can help them. But it is not your job anymore. Free yourself.

If you live your own life in happiness, seeking it out at every turn, finding ways to feel good, surrounding yourself with good and supportive people, you will not become like the complainers in your life that you can't stand being around.

Do not feel guilty. Guilt is a negative emotion. It is tough to let guilt go, especially if the complainers in your life are close to you and insist on being heard. Keep trying to release the guilt that they are so good at piling on you.

Listen to uplifting music, meditate, and say positive affirmations to yourself throughout the day.

Here's one I love that I heard on a Deepak Chopra meditation series:

I am a wonderful person.
I am a beautiful person.
I love myself,
Exactly as I am.

Be positive. Be proactive, be grateful, appreciative, give compliments, and look for the good. Be nice. Open your heart, be vulnerable, go with the flow of life, let love enter, and for goodness sakes, no complaining.

ADVICE I THOUGHT
I'D NEVER GIVE

As the head of an executive search & strategic consulting practice, I give advice all of the time.

I give advice to friends, family, and acquaintances. I give advice to job seekers who want to land the job of their dreams and I give advice to companies on how to run a better cultural environment so that they can keep their employees from leaving.

I listen to many stories and, based on years of experience and education, I make an informed judgment call as to what I believe to be the best scenario for each situation.

For example, I recently advised a professional from an Ivy League college who wanted to get out of his current job. He worked close to 100 hours a week and had no life. He saw his newborn son for half an hour a day, mostly when the boy was asleep. The guy was miserable, so we moved him to a firm where his stress level plummeted and his free time increased. Sometimes we have to look beyond money.

I counseled a woman working for a top university, who held a high paying position, about choosing the most important quality of life to her. Was it money, title, family? Her choice could affect her promotion down the road. She was at a point where she was second guessing everything in her work and life. She quit a month later to start a family.

I guided a young Vice President to stay where he was for two more years, even though I knew his skills and experience were an ideal match for a position I was filling. I also was quite sure that if he took the role, he would appear to be job-hopping. This would haunt him in the future.

I spend time interviewing employees at leading companies to figure out why their people are jumping ship. In one case, I discovered that a division boss was a bully and micro-manager, yet everyone was afraid to speak up because he controlled compensation. I encouraged a key human resources figure inside the company to detail the complaints to the leaders of the firm. Since then, the company has completely reorganized. I no longer get weekly calls from employees inside the firm begging me to get them out of there. This saved the company millions in recruiting, on boarding, retention costs, and potential lost revenues.

I am a realist and I am honest about the unspoken truths of the job market from both sides of the table. I do my best to give practical and strategic advice that helps people get ahead or companies beat the competition by keeping top talent engaged.

> *"While I primarily help experienced professionals and well-known companies, I recently found myself in a situation where I had to give the kind of advice that went against everything I believed…and I had to give it to my son."*

I flew from San Francisco to Florida to watch my son play in a NCAA tennis tournament, where winning college teams throughout the country are invited to compete. He lost his singles and doubles matches the day I arrived.

I sat quietly in the 90-degree heat and hardwood bleachers, doing my best to appear unaffected as he walked away from the courts to a distant picnic table with his head and shoulders practically dragging on the ground. It took all I had not to follow him.

After about 10 minutes, teammates made their way over one-by-one, said a word or two to him, and left. It was like a choreographed dance. Their timing was just right. This was a real team and they cared.

Eventually, my son got up, walked toward me, climbed up the stands, and sat very close.

"Hi Mom. Thanks for coming." He hugged me briefly and put his head in his hands. Silence.

After several minutes of nothing, he began to speak in a hushed tone. Words just fell out of his mouth, out of his heart.

"I hate my life. I hate school. I hate the pressure. I hate my routine: I go to class, study, practice, study, play matches, study, sleep, and do it all over again. Every day. I hate losing matches. I am not at the top of my class. I am a failure. I have no idea what I am going to do with my life. Why did I major in economics? What does an economics major do anyway? I need an internship this summer. This is the summer I'm supposed to have one, the summer before my senior year, and I don't. How will I make money? How will I get a job after college? I don't want to teach tennis again this summer. I don't want to be a lawyer like Dad. I don't know what I want to do. What do I do?"

I was at a loss for the first time in my professional and motherly life, but random thoughts were racing.

Please don't fall apart. Life isn't that bad. You have had many struggles and even more successes. You just have to continue to work hard, to show up. You are a naturally likeable person, just keep your nose to the grindstone. Your hormones are changing at this age, so everything seems worse than it is. Talk to your professors. Reach out to alumni. Do informational interviews when you're not studying or playing tennis (which is never). You're not a quitter. Start worrying because I surely am.

I left those words in my head.

"One thing I know for sure about raising children is that every single day a kid needs discipline...But also every single day a kid needs a break."
—**Anne Lamott**, *Bird by Bird: Some Instructions on Writing and Life*

I live just over the Golden Gate Bridge from San Francisco, and I often see Anne Lamott when hiking along trails in Marin. I have always admired how relaxed she seems, so in touch with life and nature and what really matters. I have read several of her books about life. They're all from the heart. And so, like Anne, I eventually let go and let my heart speak.

"I noticed that each of your teammates came over to talk to you after your matches."

"Yeah. They are good guys."

"Boy, to have friends like that in life, it doesn't get much better." He just looked at me. No lecture? No analysis? No pep talk? No "let me fix this for you"?

"Did you meet any of my teammates?" I think he wasn't sure where to take the conversation.

"Actually, every one of your teammates came up and introduced himself to me while you were playing. I was impressed."

"Yeah. We pride ourselves on being gentlemen."

"It's an admirable quality to have. It made me proud to be sitting on your team's bench." He smiled and I continued gently.

"You know, maybe you just need a breather." My son's head whipped around.

"What?!" I did my best to appear at ease.

"Have you thought about traveling this summer; just giving yourself a break and seeing what comes up?"

It was quiet again. *Did I blow it?* And then...

"Actually, that's what my friend from Princeton did last summer. He had no idea what he wanted to do either, so he decided to travel around the world. He said it was the best thing he ever did. He has always had huge expectations put on him and he wanted to figure life out for himself. I've been thinking of doing the same thing."

"Awesome!" And that was the end of conversation.

What made me want to just go with the flow at that moment, rather than follow my usual way of analyzing, solving, and fixing? Somehow, I just knew in my heart that if my son had some relief from the ongoing pressure, long enough to gain his own perspective, he would find happiness.

It takes courage to shift from our comfort zone and go to a place that, if we are really honest with ourselves, we know to be true and right:

If you are in need of a shift in your work or life, keep these takeaways in mind:

- Relax, breathe, and believe in the process.
- Give yourself time and space to figure it out. It's not your fault if you don't know yet.
- It's okay not to have the perfect answer at the perfect moment.
- Encourage yourself.
- Listen to your heart over your head.
- Leave your high expectations at the door.
- Silence and contemplation can be your best advisors, use them.

Finally, as I continue to counsel experienced individuals like you and me, professionals and corporations, I know one thing for sure: I am going to put happiness at the center in the advice business.

When we are happy in our careers and in our lives, amazing things can happen.

LIVE YOUR FAIRYTALE

What exactly is a fairytale?

Is it the perfect fantasy that we read about in children's books like *Cinderella*, *Snow White,* or *Rapunzel,* or see in movies like *Ever After, Shrek* and *Lord of the Rings*?

Fairytales are quickly disregarded because people think they are unattainable. Marry the prince or princess (many of us live with a broken heart), rule the world (some people don't get out of the mailroom), become beautiful (we are not all supermodels), be the hero and save the world (even Bill Gates, who has a lot of money and is trying to eradicate polio, can't save the world).

Yet, if we consider the structure and path of a fairytale and apply it to our own lives, suddenly it doesn't seem so far off. We can get there. Don't we all deserve a fairytale life?

But how do you do that? Both in your work *and* in your personal life?

According to a research paper written by Bette U. Kiernan, MFT, of MIT on the use of fairytales by psychologists like Carl Jung, the fairytale is often a hero's journey, which is an archetype, or representation of the sharing of the collective thoughts and issues that we deal with in our own lives. We all want many of the same things. We want to figure our lives out, to achieve, to be happy. A fairytale enables us to become part of a grander, unified consciousness. We relate and we connect with others. This is the essence of a fairytale and its usefulness for the good of all. It is happiness.

Step one is finding where we belong. Part of this journey is the journey itself. What's included in that journey are the key elements of a fairytale:

- Your current world isn't *all that.*
- You are introduced to a new world or you get curious and explore until you find what you want your world to be.
- You jump into your new world (experience, job, relationship).
- It is going well and then it isn't.
- But then, after learning, exploring, committing, using intuition, and determination, you end up happier because you allow yourself to dig deep until you reach the point where you say...
- "This is great! I love my life, my job, my relationship, myself."
- Or not.

If not, then go back to the beginning and do it again.

Take President Abraham Lincoln for instance:

- 1816 - His family was forced out of their home. He had to work to support them.
- 1818 - His mother died.
- 1831 - Failed in business.
- 1832 - Ran for state legislature and lost. Also lost his job. And wanted to go to law school but couldn't get in.
- 1833 - Borrowed some money from a friend to begin a business and by the end of the year he was bankrupt. He spent the next 17 years of his life paying off this debt.
- 1834 - Ran for state legislature again and won.
- 1835 – Was engaged to be married, sweetheart died, and his heart was broken.
- 1836 - Had a total nervous breakdown and was in bed for six months.

- 1838 - Sought to become speaker of the state legislature, but was defeated.
- 1840 - Sought to become elector, but was defeated.
- 1843 - Ran for Congress and lost.
- 1846 - Ran for Congress again and won. Moved to Washington and did a great job.
- 1848 - Ran for re-election to Congress and lost.
- 1849 - Sought the job of land officer in his home state and was rejected.
- 1854 - Ran for Senate of the United States and lost.
- 1856 - Sought the Vice-Presidential nomination at his party's national convention and got less than 100 votes.
- 1858 - Ran for U.S. Senate again and lost.
- 1860 - Elected president of the United States.

Abraham Lincoln is the classic fairytale. I bet you didn't know that.

From my perspective, the most important ingredient to living your own fairytale—the one thing you must do in order to achieve true happiness and love your life:

Never, ever, ever, give up.
Never, ever, ever.
Never, ever.
Never.
Never give up.

That's it. You will prevail. If you keep at it, from my perspective, you can live a fairytale and a life of happiness every day.

What could be better?

MEET SOMEONE NEW EVERY DAY

A 6-Day Experiment

Recently a friend sent me the summary of a book called A Curious Mind--The Secret to a Bigger Life by Brian Grazer and Charles Fishman.

I like the word 'curious' because I am the curious type, which is why I am writing my current book, *SHIFT,* highlighting stories of people who have found true meaning in their work and in their life.

In *A Curious Mind*, Grazer writes that he is best friends with Ron Howard. He just called Ron up—well, Grazer was already a well-known movie producer so Ron was probably open to taking his call. He also writes about conversations with other famous people like Princess Diana and Barack Obama when he was a Senator.

While I am not a famous person, I like having conversations with people I don't know, yet. Writers tend to be curious and pay attention to their environment. We seek out new experiences whenever we can.

Many years ago I was walking down a back hallway in a building in New York City when I ran into Muhammed Ali and his bodyguard. It was just the three of us. I said, *"Hello Mr. Ali."* He stopped, slowly leaned forward, gave me a hug, and then asked me (in slowly constructed words) if I wanted his autograph. I gladly accepted the invitation, but only had a napkin to write on. I still have his autograph. When I learned that he had passed, I remembered the napkin that I put in one of my scrapbooks, and smiled as I remembered our brief exchange.

———◆———

Last week, a young worker for a local internet provider came over to set up an internet connection for me. He had giant red bulbs hanging from each ear. As previously mentioned, I like to engage in conversations with new people, so I commented on them.

"I like your earrings. They remind me of people who put giant rings in their ears to increase the size of the holes." But as I looked closer, I saw that I was wrong.

"They're not earrings," he replied. Oops. I hoped that I hadn't offended him. (When you reach out sometimes, the foot goes in mouth). I figured that since I had started the conversation, I needed to finish it.

"Oh, what are they?"

"They are from years of boxing."

"Can you remove them?"

"No."

"Well, I think they look like cool earrings. So, let me show you where the router goes."

"Thanks. I kind of like them. Reminds me of my love for boxing."

I thought about my visit with Muhammed, who was a world champion boxer and, while he had a slowing of brain and body movement, he didn't have the ear bulbs. I was curious and so I looked up the condition.

Cauliflower ear: An acquired deformity of the external ear to which wrestlers and boxers are particularly vulnerable, due to trauma.

When a blood clot (hematoma) forms under the skin of the ear, the
clot disrupts the connection of the skin to the ear cartilage.

Maybe that will be a trait of one of the characters in a future book. He made it into this article, so you never know.

———◆———

A few months ago, I was in a bookstore and noticed that the cashier had a giant tattoo on his neck that read, *God is Dead.* I was curious.

"Wow, cool tattoo! Why that phrase?"

"Because he is."

Interesting.

———◆———

I was in line at the grocery store the other day and noticed that the woman in front of me was wolfing down chocolate covered raisins (that she had bagged from the bulk bin) so that she didn't have to pay for them all (or she was really hungry). As she swiped her credit card to pay for the groceries, it was obvious that her mouth was full of (and drooling) the chocolate covered raisins. What was the checker going to do? Ask her to spit them out so that they could be weighed and then charge her for them? Accuse her, humiliate her, or just let it go? He let it go and smiled the whole time. He was a giver.

Interesting.

———◆———

So after reading the summary of *A Curious Mind* and keenly observing the world around me on a daily basis, I decided that I would try an experiment. I would commit to meeting someone new every day for six days and, if the situation warranted, have a meaningful conversation. Why six days? I wanted a day off to reflect.

A Summary of Who I Met and What I Learned

Day 1

I was out with friends, one of whom invited another friend to join us. The guy was the owner of a local gym. Not the sweatshop type, but a low key gym where people from all walks of life go. People worth millions work alongside others hovering above the poverty line, but are invested in their bodies anyway.

The gym owner was going through a tough divorce, which basically meant he was starting over, and in the next breath told me that I should meet his spitfire girlfriend who teaches Pilates (something I have always wanted to try because I need a stronger core). He had the biggest smile and the shiniest head. I liked him right away.

I later reflected on how happy the guy was, even though his life behind the scenes was a challenge. He was engaged in the moment. We all have roadblocks along the way; it's how we react to them that helps establish our quality of life.

Day 2

I met his girlfriend, the Pilates Instructor, and took my first lesson. She was a high energy dynamo and a cancer survivor-twice! I watched her say goodbye to the client before me. She offered a big hug, a sincere smile, and a few words of encouragement to the person, which went beyond getting in shape. She knew how to connect with people. I could tell that she had compassion, empathy, and a zest for life.

During my lesson she was so attentive to me and I learned that she had a lack of concern about what anyone thought about her. She was full of great ideas to help others (not just cancer survivors) and had already befriended a homeless man who told her that she saved his life by being his friend.

After my very cool session with her (oh, I signed up for 8 more), I thought about how much I really respected this gal and, heck, she can do and say whatever she darn well pleases. I mean, to go through cancer, a divorce, raise three kids, run a business, and be happy. That's embracing life and living it. She may be in a future book, too!

Day 3

I was out to dinner with a friend and we ran into some acquaintances at a cool restaurant where we showed up, hoping to get a seat at the bar. There weren't any available and the hostess told us that we could maybe get in at 10 p.m.

Lucky for us we ran into the newer friends and were able to snag two seats at the community table where several of their friends were sitting. They told us that they were hosting a party for yet another friend and that we could join them.

We declined because we didn't want to intrude, but they did introduce us to a bunch of new people, one of whom was surfer Shaun Tomson. I said hi and shook his hand, not knowing who he was, until the friend I was with knew who he was and whispered, "I wish I could have gotten my picture with him."

Not long after we said our goodbyes and took our community table seats, Shaun pulled up a chair and visited with us for a good half hour while we ate our meal. He and my friend talked about surfing and family and life in general. I found out that Shaun was from South Africa (loved his accent), but I mostly listened and concluded that he is a nice, casual guy. He left us by pointing at my friend and saying "You are a good man and you are with your sweetheart." How sweet. I gave him a big hug when we all got up to leave.

Being the curious type, later that night I looked him up. I discovered that he was a world champion surfer, had a clothing line and gave lots of speeches to large corporations about the things that we all should do in life to be successful and happy. You can watch one of his speeches at on YouTube. Interesting!

Day 4

I got a massage by a guy who was hippy-like and very mellow. I liked him right away and noticed the giant holes in his earlobes. Reminded me of the internet worker, both with their unique ears.

What inspired me about the masseuse was his soft-spoken nature, his simple approach to life, the fact that he had worked at Esalen Institute in Big Sur, California, for years (an institute I knew many teachers from). I immediately thought back to the three days I spent in silence at a monastery down the road from Esalen in an attempt to figure out my own life path.

The masseuse was at peace and completely content spending an hour and a half working his craft and offering healing to another. Selfless, calm, content. He was living a life of happiness.

Day 5

I went running with a new gal I had met on several occasions. She drove me to a trail high above the ocean, which we could see in the distance. I felt like I was on top of the world. The run was magical. A large black and yellow butterfly crossed in front of me. I told her that I see a butterfly every day.

We navigated our way up and down fire roads and single tracks until we covered 8.5 miles. I was so enjoying our girl time conversation, that I didn't even notice how far we had travelled.

We talked about everything: relationships, work/life balance, our dreams, our feelings. There was no judgment, no competition. I later reflected on that interaction and realized that having girlfriends, having friends in general, is so important for a happy, balanced life. We all have so much on our plate, but to take the time to connect in meaningful, heartfelt conversation is a way to replenish the soul. It was a great morning.

Day 6

I was sitting alone at a bar in a restaurant where I was waiting to meet a colleague. Even though I am not the bar type, I am okay with being alone. I had my iPhone with me, which has all sorts of books loaded onto it, and I could check my email. Otherwise, when I am alone in a new place, I like to observe.

A woman took the seat next to me. Great opportunity to strike up a conversation. I found out that she was new to the area and wanted to go to a newcomer mixer the following week and that, maybe, I would like to go with her. She was a criminal defense attorney, her son recently graduated from an Ivy League college and now lived in New York and she missed him greatly. She dreamed about having a place in New York, so she could see him more often. We talked about her work/life balance, her desire to make new friends, and her love for her son. I told her that we had both made a new friend.

And then my colleague showed up and she was gone. I think I'll probably run into her again at a newcomer mixer.

Day 7
Today is Day 7. I think I will continue my experiment. I have a funny feeling that I will meet someone very interesting.

My 6-Day Conversation Takeaways

- Live in the moment
- Be empathetic
- Listen and learn
- Smile
- Do not judge
- Be curious
- Reach out, talk to people
- Be a giver
- Do your own thing
- Happiness is about connecting with others

ABOUT THE AUTHOR

Jody B. Miller is CEO of C2C Executive Search & Strategic Consulting, a corporate job placement and employment consultation firm, which puts her in contact with thousands of people and their stories. She is a Career and Life Coach and has helped thousands of people find meaning and happiness in their work and in their lives.

Jody's prior positions include being the Founder and President of Ceres Ad Systems, a media technology company; a Sales & Marketing Executive for CBS Television in New York City; a Strategic Growth Consultant for Fortune 100 companies; an Investment Banker for Pacific Crest Securities; Assistant Producer of the award-winning PBS series "Traveling Lite"; and Co-founder of Dedication to Special Education, a non-profit that raises money for special needs children in grades K-12. Jody also created and hosted the cable TV series, "Living Young."

She is a regular contributor to *LinkedIn*, *The Huffington Post*, and Ignite's *Financial Times* magazine. She writes articles about job satisfaction, work/life balance, and finding meaning.

Jody graduated from the University of California at Santa Barbara with a dual Bachelor's degree in communications and sociology. Her education gave her additional perspective as to the many ways we communicate with ourselves and with one another in our search for happiness and meaning in work and in life. She has also taken courses on creativity from The Venture Lab at Stanford University.

Her curiosity and engagement in the world around her drives her to hear and write about people's stories—stories that challenge, inspire, and transform. *FROM DRIFT to SHIFT* gives readers the ability to do just that—to their perspective and live a work and personal life of true meaning and happiness.

Jody splits her time between Southern and Northern California.

For more information about the author, visit www.jodybmiller.com.

Morgan James makes all of our titles available
through the Library for All Charity Organizations.

www.LibraryForAll.org

Printed in the USA
CPSIA information can be obtained
at www.ICGtesting.com
JSHW022214140824
68134JS00018B/1056

9 781683 502920